T0043065

EVERYDAY ACTIVISM

EVERYDAY ACTIVISM

HOW TO CHANGE THE WORLD
IN **FIVE MINUTES, ONE HOUR** OR **A DAY**

RACHEL ENGLAND

HarperCollins*Publishers*

HarperCollins*Publishers*
1 London Bridge Street
London SE1 9GF

www.harpercollins.co.uk

HarperCollins*Publishers*
1st Floor, Watermarque Building, Ringsend Road
Dublin 4, Ireland

First published by HarperCollins*Publishers* 2021

1 3 5 7 9 10 8 6 4 2

A catalogue record of this book is
available from the British Library

ISBN 978-0-00-843411-3

Printed and bound in Great Britain by
CPI Group (UK) Ltd, Croydon

This book is produced from independently certified FSC™ paper
to ensure responsible forest management

For more information visit: www.harpercollins.co.uk/green

CONTENTS

INTRODUCTION

Let's face it, the planet is not in a good way at the moment. Unless you've spent the last several decades hiding in a cave (and who would blame you?), it can't have escaped your notice that things in general aren't in the greatest state. Scientists are issuing increasingly stark warnings about changes in the climate, human rights across many parts of the world seem to be moving backwards instead of forwards and years of political ignorance have only served to highlight huge discrepancies in equality and justice across the board. It all paints a depressing picture!

But what's to be done about it all? What difference can we, as individuals, really make? It's a question we've all asked ourselves: simply, what's the point in trying to rectify these huge problems? We can't all be Greta Thunberg or Malala Yousafzai, after all, so it's easy to sink into futility and grudgingly accept that 'this is just how things are'.

This is the problem with thinking on such a grand scale – it can be debilitating. The larger the goal – preventing climate change, ending racial bias, achieving human rights for all – the greater the change that's needed and the less we believe we're capable of achieving it. Smaller goals, however – more manageable actions – now *they're* doable, but do they have any impact?

Yes! They do. Because every time we think our own little actions don't matter, we're not alone in having that thought. It's important to remember that there are seven billion of us on this planet and when just *some* of us take these small steps, big things *can* happen. As life is so online these days, when enough voices come together, the capitalist giants who, sadly, run this world have no choice but to listen to us.

Companies and brands are more responsive to people power in this digital age – they're sensitive to public pressure and want to preserve their reputations. So when big pockets of their customer base (aka their income stream) start making a fuss about something, they can't ignore it. In 2018, for example, a bunch of US airlines, car rental companies and hotel chains announced they would no longer be offering special deals or discounts to members of the National Rifle Association (NRA) following lobbying from gun-control advocates. Granted, it wasn't an earth-shattering move, but it sent an important message amid America's ongoing firearm problem, so it was a step in the right direction – and it simply wouldn't have happened without people power. It wasn't just one person who drove that change – it was thousands, all writing letters, raising awareness and voting with their wallets.

The same is true of designer jewellery brand Cartier, which vowed to drop Myanmar's 'genocide gems' following a sustained boycott campaign against the company in 2017. Ditto SeaWorld, which ended its captive orca breeding programmes in 2016 following public pressure, and Nestlé, which in 2010 promised a zero-deforestation policy in its palm-oil supply chain after Greenpeace's awareness campaigns sparked massive global outcry. In 2010, meanwhile, wholesale garment maker Fruit of the Loom crumbled in the face of an enormous student boycott, reopening a Honduran factory it had closed after its workers had unionised. Incredibly, the brand also gave all 1,200 employees their jobs back, awarded them $2.5 million in compensation and restored all union rights. That's people power in action.

These are all examples of major global campaigns, but the inspirational and motivational impact of their success can't be underestimated. If activism can take on the likes of Nestlé, then it can certainly take on smaller Goliaths. Plans for a proposed coal power plant in the Turkish village of Yirca, for example, were scrapped in 2014 when residents mobilised to save the olive groves that would be destroyed in its development. In 2015, in the Sussex village of Balcombe, a sustained and well-televised campaign against fracking led to the creation of community-owned clean energy initiative REPOWER Balcombe. There are many, many more examples of successful collective action on a local level throughout the world.

And there is proven theory to back this up. A Harvard University research paper by political scientist Erica Chenoweth indicates that it takes around 3.5 per cent of a population to actively participate in a protest to drive meaningful political change.[1] On a national level, that's still a lot – around 2.3 million people in the UK (roughly twice the size of Birmingham) or 11 million in the US (more than the population of New York City). But on a local level and in smaller communities, which are often more cohesive, that '3.5 per cent rule' is much more practicable.

Of course, it's easy to wax lyrical about this kind of people power when everyone is working towards a tangible goal – when an objective can be achieved and the issue finally resolved with a campaign win or a company's change of tack. But the very sprawling and unwieldy nature of our biggest challenges – mitigating climate change, addressing human rights imbalances, and so on – means that on an individual level, we often can't see the impact or outcome of our behaviours. Out of which comes the 'why bother?' dilemma. But again, we have to remember that none of us is going to save the world single-handedly (probably). Change – whether we can see it or not – comes from everyone playing their part.

Take the incredibly dull job of doing the laundry, for example. Line-drying your clothes outside during the summer, instead of using a tumble dryer, will save around £30 a year on your electricity bill and 90kg in CO_2 emissions.[2] These are fairly shrug-worthy sums, but if everyone in the UK did this, the emissions saved would be the equivalent of taking 397,154 cars off the road.[3] *That's* significant. Some people respond well to these kinds of comparisons – it helps them visualise the impact their actions are making, and even difficult-to-quantify behaviours come with hard numbers. Online initiative Good & Kind (goodandkind.org), for example, has conducted tireless research into the inherent cost benefit to society of lots of everyday actions. Buying milk from a local dairy, for example, benefits society by £3.12. Taking simple steps to prevent loneliness in older people benefits society by £47.80. Planting flowers for bees, meanwhile, racks up a whopping £4,819.28 (more on bees on page 34).

But let's forget statistics and numbers for a minute. What it all ultimately comes down to is not 'why?' but rather 'why not?' Especially since – as you'll see in this book – there are so many things you can do to help make the world a better place that don't require much effort at all. And if we all do them, change in all metrics can and will happen. There is strength in numbers, particularly in this digital life where people can share their thoughts and beliefs with potentially huge audiences easily and instantly, and – as trust in brands and more traditional institutions like media or government nosedives – when people are increasingly making decisions based on the influence of their peers and others like them.

This book is split into three sections: five-minute quick wins, actions in an hour and jobs for a day. They are all specific and actionable – you won't find any vague or generic suggestions here – and they cover all aspects of everyday life. And they're realistic. 'Eradicate plastic from your home' is a great idea in theory, but is it achievable? Not really. Can you make sure you're properly recycling the plastic you *do* use (see pages 41–2)? Yes. Not every suggestion will be applicable to everyone, of course, and some might already be part of your lifestyle, so choose the ones that will make a meaningful difference in your day-to-day life. Then spread the word about your efforts. Tweet about your lower energy bills (see pages 68–9), Instagram your veggie dinner (see pages 63–6) and talk your mate's ear off about how much money you made car-booting your junk (see pages 99–100). Inspire, encourage and motivate – *that's* the real work to be done. And remember, small acts in big amounts are a force to be reckoned with. One wasp at a picnic is annoying, but a swarm is a game-changer. Let's create a swarm.

IF YOU
HAVE FIVE
MINUTES ...

1. SIGN A PETITION

Petition-signing is often castigated by critics as the ultimate form of so-called 'slacktivism', and in many ways that's a fair assessment. All it takes is a few clicks, there's little personal investment or risk involved, and signatories get that lovely warm feeling of having done something proactive when, really, they've not done much at all. And it's disheartening that so few petitions – even the massive millions-strong endeavours that make headline news – fail to enact any tangible change.

But petitions make an impact in other ways that shouldn't be underestimated. People like to feel included in the social norm, so seeing a friend or family member sign and share a petition on social media can prompt an internal dialogue: 'If Sarah cares about this cause, should I?' Whether or not they actually sign the petition after seeing Sarah do so is less important than the thought it's sparked in someone who might not have considered the cause in question otherwise. Perhaps they'll reflect on the matter some more, read up on it, chat to others about it. This is how awareness is created (just a heads-up, awareness is going to be mentioned a lot in this book).

Signing a petition also sends a message to lawmakers and authorities. Even if they choose not to respond with any kind of direct action, it serves as a reasonably strong indication of popular consensus. More than 1.86 million people in the UK signed a petition in 2017 calling for the cancellation of US President Donald Trump's state visit. The memorable event went ahead nonetheless, but when Trump and his team stepped off *Air Force One* they did so knowing that they weren't welcome by everyone.

Finally, petitions serve as a practical way for movement organisers to gather useful data about their support base. Most petition sites ask for your postcode, for example. This tells organisers which pockets of the country are receptive to their ideas and potential further action, as well as areas where a different kind of approach may be needed.

A petition might not change anything on its own, but as part of the wider activism jigsaw it can help provide a solid and useful foundation for a cause. Many governments around the world have their own official petition portals (petition.parliament.uk and petitions.whitehouse.gov, for example), while sites such as Change.org, Avaaz.org and 38Degrees.org.uk are popular campaigning platforms open to everyone for a huge range of causes on both a local and international level.

2. CHANGE YOUR SEARCH ENGINE

We rely on the internet for a *lot*, and having the sum total of human knowledge at our fingertips means that search engines receive billions of queries every single day around the world. From simple queries such as 'How do I boil an egg?' to more complex existential ponderings on the likes of life, death and the universe, 'I'll just google that' has become a *de facto* response to just about any question the human mind can pose.

And indeed, Google is the go-to search engine, accounting for 82.41 per cent of search-engine market share in 2019[4] and churning through 3.5 billion questions a day[5] – that's more than 1.2 trillion queries a year. This all adds up to a *big* chunk of ad revenue for the tech giant – in 2019, the company made almost $134.8 billion from revenue associated with the adverts placed on every page of its search results.[6]

Of course, while the likes of competitors such as Yahoo and Bing are very keen for a slice of that pie, so are contenders that have more principled objectives. Ethical search engines such as YouCare, EveryClick, Ecosia and Ekoru are taking Google's money-making search model and turning it on its head, siphoning off a sizeable portion of the ad revenue generated by searches on their platforms and donating it to charity and good causes. Ecosia, for example, uses its profits to plant trees, while Ekoru donates 60 per cent of its revenue to ocean clean-up initiatives around the globe.

Other search-engine alternatives, meanwhile, let you decide how your internet browsing can do some good in the world. YouCare, for example, turns your searches into meals for animals in shelters and support for researchers investigating cancer treatment, while EveryClick backs a range of charities and claims to have helped raise more than £12.5 million since its launch in 2005.[7] What's more, most of these more ethical alternatives have a completely transparent approach to the way they operate and take meaningful steps to offset their carbon activity, so the only kind of impact they have on the world is the good kind!

3. MAKE A MICRO-DONATION

'Give money to charity' might not be the most imaginative suggestion for driving positive change, but for a lot of people charitable giving conjures up images of tedious Direct Debit forms and ongoing financial commitments. Due to various tech innovations and open banking reforms, though, giving to good causes is easier and more pain-free than ever before thanks to the emerging trend of micro-donations.

Instead of pledging to give a charity a set amount of money every month, micro-donation platforms work on a 'little and often' principle that digitally mimics old-school charity boxes on shop counters. Apps such as Sustainably and Roundups in the UK, and GiveTide and Coin Up in the US, work by linking securely to your bank account and then rounding up the spare pennies from every purchase you make on a credit or debit card. Spent £3.75 on your morning coffee? These types of apps will round that up to £4 (or to the nearest 10p or 50p depending on the app and your settings) and donate that extra 25p to the charity of your choice. Obviously, 25p is not a life-changing sum for anyone involved, but if 50,000 people – the population of a medium-sized town – did that three times a week, that's £150,000 for charity in a month, or £1.8 million in a year.

Micro-donations don't rely solely on smartphone apps, either. Pennies From Heaven is a long-established scheme for employers that allows staff to donate the spare change from their weekly or monthly payslips, while Pennies.org.uk is a platform that allows shoppers to make one-off round-up donations to charity at the checkout, either on a retailer's website or via the card machine if the customer is in-store. Pennies says that its platform alone has raised more than £24 million for charity since the launch, and that we could raise as much as £1 billion every year if every adult in the UK gave just 35p a week.[8] So you don't have to give a wedge of cash to charity to make it count – a little change can change a lot.

4. TURN YOUR ONLINE SHOPPING INTO FREE DONATIONS

They say money makes the world go around and it's no secret that in a society largely driven by capitalism there are a fair few companies out there with enough cash in the bank to put a significant dent in the world's ills. But that's a different book.

Ideally, we'd all just boycott these big brands, but doing so would require a major overhaul, not only in our personal lifestyles, but in the wider capitalist structure, which probably isn't something we can achieve in five minutes.

However, if you do shop with the megacorps (and sometimes needs must), there are ways you can ensure that they siphon off some of their enormous wealth to causes in need – albeit in small amounts.

In 2018, an estimated 1.8 billion people bought goods online, with global retail sales amounting to a whopping $2.8 trillion – a figure that's only going to get bigger.[9] Most of us use the internet to shop for items in one way or another, whether it's for clothes and cosmetics, furniture, groceries or little odds and ends like greetings cards. And you can turn every purchase you make into a donation to a cause of your choice by using one of the increasingly popular charitable giving websites or extensions that are popping up all over the web – at no extra cost to you.

Amazon brought the idea mainstream with its AmazonSmile platform. Operated by Amazon, the website offers exactly the same products, prices and shopping features as the usual Amazon site, but when you shop through the Smile channel, Amazon donates 0.5 per cent of the net purchase price to a good cause of your choice. Other sites, such as Altruisto, The Giving Machine, Give as you Live and Giving Assistant, operate in the same way, except instead of one single retailer, they've partnered with dozens of household brands. All you need to do is sign up and then shop online as you normally would. The associated companies, which can include the likes of Argos,

Groupon, eBay, ASOS and Booking.com (depending on which platform you use), will then make a donation to your choice of charity every time you shop with them.

This is big retail's way of 'giving back', and yes, the money they contribute is extremely stingy compared to the amount they're making every year. But it's money nonetheless, and you don't have to do anything to get them to part with it except do your shopping as usual. And, as is the case with micro-donations (see pages 13–14), it all adds up. According to easyfundraising.co.uk, for example, its members have raised more than £32 million for good causes since the site launched in 2005.[10]

5. SUPPORT AN INDEPENDENT BUSINESS

Indie businesses come in all shapes and forms, from the single artisan jewellery maker to the chain of coffee shops spread across a town, and whatever their wares, they all have one thing in common: they're born of love and passion.

In a world that's increasingly homogenised, independent businesses provide originality and variety, and have a real and impactful effect on community cohesion. They're run by people, not boards, and when you support an independent business, you're directly helping owners to put food on the table (and not, in the case of many multinationals, helping them dodge their tax liabilities – but again, that's a completely separate book).

Independent businesses are also a major economic driver. Small and medium-sized businesses in the UK account for around three-fifths of the country's employment,[11] and for every £1 spent with a small or medium-sized business, an estimated 63p stays in the local economy, compared to 40p with a larger business.[12] Plus, they're kinder on the environment, with research showing that materials and logistics used by local shops often have a much lower carbon footprint than the bigger brands.[13]

But indie businesses are economically vulnerable. With razor-thin profit margins and constant competition with more cash-rich chain companies, their existence is often a tightrope walk, so if you want that lovely craft shop or super-reliable handyman to be in business in three months' time, you need to support them now.

Obviously, the best way to do this is to buy their goods and pay for their service. But that's not always feasible. Not everyone has the budget for things beyond the necessities, and some services – plumbing or decorating, for example – are used on more of an ad-hoc basis. But there are other ways to show your support. Some indie creators take small one-off donations using platforms such as Ko-fi or Tipeee, for example, so you can help them out without committing to a big spend.

Hype, meanwhile, costs nothing. Say you visit a swish bakery and take an arty shot of a cupcake for the 'gram, and then someone in your social circle – who just happens to be organising a baby shower – sees the pic and makes an enquiry. Bam – you've essentially given that company a party's worth of custom. The same applies to Google and Yelp reviews – a good review is invaluable to a small business and could be the very thing to push a big spender into making a call.

6. LOOK AT THE LABEL

Depending on your penchant for dawdling crowds and artificial lighting, doing the weekly food shop is either an enjoyable jaunt out of the house or an endurance exercise in mental resilience. In either case, it's a necessary event – and it's one where you can make a real difference to your carbon footprint without having to do much at all.

The food industry as a whole is responsible for between 20–30 per cent of global greenhouse gas emissions.[14] It's a complicated system comprising numerous facets, such as transport and logistics, agriculture, processing, packaging and so on, and there are multiple international schemes and commitments in place to encourage manufacturers and suppliers to take action on this hefty carbon debt.

But the end consumer can play their part by making smarter shopping choices around what they buy and when they buy it. Transporting food around the UK, for example, accounts for nearly 25 per cent of all trips made by heavy goods vehicles every year – air freighting food, meanwhile, accounts for 11 per cent of the total carbon emissions from UK food transport.[15] Buying food produced locally, then, can help to mitigate the impact of these food miles. In fact, some reports suggest that if we all only bought food originating from within a 20km radius from our homes, the country would save over £2 billion in congestion and environmental costs.[16]

And while the debate around organic produce rages on, environmental experts do largely agree that if you're able to (and organic produce is no longer as prohibitively expensive as it once was), you should go for organic as it's the more eco-friendly choice. Why? Organic farming helps create a healthy living soil that's more resistant to drought, flooding and consequently the impacts of climate change. Plus, organic farmers select crop varieties with natural resistance to particular pests and diseases, which reduces the need to use chemicals.

The next time you're standing in front of a veg display or meat chiller (more on meat consumption on pages 63–5), take a cursory glance at the item's packaging for its place of origin and any accreditation symbols, such as the Soil Association symbol in the UK (denoting organic produce) or the Fair Trade logo (which guarantees that the item, even if from overseas, has been produced in a sustainable fashion). If it works for your shopping list and/or budget, making a simple switch can make a meaningful difference.

7. BUY AN EXTRA ITEM AT THE SUPERMARKET FOR A FOOD BANK

Food banks have taken on a renewed focus in recent years, with more people relying on them to feed themselves and their families than ever before. In the UK alone, some 14 million people are living in poverty, and according to hunger charity The Trussell Trust, the period between April 2018 and March 2019 saw a 19 per cent increase in the number of people requesting food parcels from their local food bank centres.[17]

The vast majority – some 90 per cent – of food distributed by food banks in the UK is donated by the public and used to create a minimum of three days' nutritionally balanced emergency food for people who have been referred in crisis. The system depends on the goodwill of those who are able to give.

Most towns and cities have a central drop-off point for food bank donations, which are a good place to head if you're having a big cupboard clear-out or want to make a more sizeable donation. But as with so many things in life, convenience is king, which is why food banks in countries around the world have partnered with supermarkets to give shoppers the chance to donate newly bought food items there and then – you'll usually find donation bins and baskets after the checkouts or near the exits. Their positioning means a lot of shoppers won't clock them until they've already done their shop, though, so pop a note on your shopping list as a reminder to pick up an item as you're perusing the aisles.

Obviously, you should only donate what you're able to, and if you're particularly skint, buy-one-get-one-free (BOGOF) deals or similar can be a good way to make a contribution without any additional cost to you. If you are in the position to make an additional purchase, though, don't just go for the failsafe beans or soup. Food banks need a variety of items to make up their parcels, not to mention non-food items such as toiletries and sanitary products (steer clear of perishables, though). Find out what your local foodbank needs at givefood.org.uk/needs or feedingamerica.org and make a note on your shopping list to add an extra item or two to your trolley next time you're at the supermarket.

8. CHOOSE A DIFFERENT TOILET ROLL

We're probably all on board with saving paper where we can, but things are a bit trickier when it comes to toilet roll. It's really the only material we can legitimately get away with using once before getting rid of it.

The average Brit gets through 127 rolls of toilet paper every year,[18] which adds up to a UK total of 1.3 million tonnes of tissue. But it's not just the paper use itself that poses an environmental problem – a huge amount of resources go into its production. A single roll of toilet paper uses around 168 litres of water to make, while manufacturing and transporting toilet roll uses 17.3 terawatts of electricity every year[19] – that's enough to charge 1.55 trillion smartphones![20]

But since going without is not really a solution (unless you're *extremely* committed, in which case, good luck), you can still make a dent in the impact of your loo roll consumption by making smarter buying choices. For a start, choose toilet roll that comes with the FSC (Forest Stewardship Council) logo on the packaging. This means the paper has come from sustainably managed forests where all trees that are cut down are replaced – see the logo for yourself on the copyright page of this book.

Or, choose toilet roll made from recycled paper. This means fewer virgin fibres (and the energy-intensive procedures needed to process them) are used per roll. Unfortunately, most of the UK's major supermarkets are actually using *less* recycled content in their own-brand toilet roll than they were a decade ago, while other popular toilet roll names are still favouring comfort and luxury over environmental credentials.[21] As such, you might consider skipping the loo roll aisle on your next big shop entirely, and opting instead for a delivery from an ethical toilet paper company.

Who Gives a Crap produces 100-per-cent recycled toilet paper (so there are no trees involved at all) and donates 50 per cent of its profits to funding sanitation projects around the world. The imaginatively titled Bumboo Company, meanwhile, makes its lux three-ply rolls from 100 per cent bamboo pulp. EcoLeaf uses 60 per cent post-consumer waste in its soft rolls, while Renova touts minimal emission and low energy consumption among the eco-friendly processes behind its chunky recycled rolls. Most of these companies will let you set up a recurring bulk order, too, so neither you nor the environment will end up being caught short on your next trip to the bathroom.

9. SWAP TO RECHARGEABLE BATTERIES

We might not be as reliant on the good ol' AA battery as we used to be, but we still get through a lot of them. In the UK alone we get rid of around 600 million disposable batteries a year and only 27 per cent of them are recycled properly – that's around 20,000 tonnes of battery waste going straight to landfill.[22] It takes around 50 times more energy to actually make a battery than the finished battery produces, too.[23]

Now, for low-drain scenarios, such as remote controls and kitchen clocks, a disposable battery will last a *long* time, so there's no major benefit in swapping to a rechargeable alternative. For high-drain uses, though, such as torches and wireless gaming controllers, making the switch can have a significant environmental benefit. Think about how frequently you end up replacing the batteries in these types of things. If you're using disposables, then your duds are just going to waste every time you're done with them. Use a rechargeable battery, however, and the resources and energy that went into creating it get spread across its multiple uses.

And there are financial advantages, too. Rechargeable batteries *are* slightly more expensive than their disposable counterparts – and obviously they require a charger – but if you're regularly forking out for new disposables, then you could save some money in the long run. Duracell claims its AAA Recharge Plus batteries can be used as many as 400 times, for example.[24] At the equivalent of around £2.50 per battery, that works out at less than a penny per use. There are some cheap disposable batteries on the market, but none that cost that little.

Something to note when you're buying rechargeable batteries: they come in different capacities. As a general rule of thumb, the lower the capacity, the less time the battery will last on a single charge. The pay-off, though, is that these types hold their charge well and won't drop in capacity even after hundreds of uses, so they'll be as effective the fiftieth time you use them as they were the first. Anything under 1,500mAh (milliampere hour) is considered low capacity for AA batteries, with 600mAh for AAA batteries.

10. DITCH FAST FASHION

It's never been easier or more affordable to be fashionable. You can pick up a new sweater for less than the price of a fancy coffee on your lunchbreak. You can order a pair of jeans online at dinnertime and they'll be delivered to your door the next morning. You can give this season's weird and wonderful trends a punt with no significant financial outlay, and when styles change – which they will at lightning speed – it's no biggie to relegate everything to the back of the closet. Assuming, that is, that it's not all fallen apart, because as with so many things, you get what you pay for.

This is all good news for the trend-following fashionista, but it's having an absolutely devastating impact on the planet, and there's an avalanche of statistics to back this up. The fashion industry produces 10 per cent of all of humanity's carbon emissions. To put that into context, that's more than international flights and maritime shipping combined.[25] It's the second-largest consumer of water worldwide,[26] with a single cotton shirt taking around 700 gallons of water to produce[27] – that's enough to give a person at least eight cups a day for *three and a half years*. And yet 85 per cent of all textiles end up in landfill every year,[28] while washing clothes releases 500,000 tons of microfibres into the ocean each year[29] – the equivalent of 50 billion plastic bottles. And we've all seen that *Blue Planet* episode.

The situation is only getting worse. Clothing production has roughly doubled since 2000,[30] with fashion chains churning out more collections per year than ever before, and while people bought 60 per cent more clothing items in 2014 than in 2000, they only kept the clothes for half as long.[31] According to the Ellen MacArthur Foundation, if the fashion sector continues on its current trajectory, its share of the carbon budget could jump to 26 per cent by 2050.[32] And these are just the environmental implications – fast fashion is also responsible for human rights violations, labour abuses and the propagation of a capitalist hierarchy that profits few at the awful expense of many.

The answer? Reduce the demand for fast fashion: stop buying it. Instead, buy better quality, well-made garments that will last, so you'll need to replace items less often. Buy from sustainable brands that are transparent about their environmental footprint and supply chains (see how your fave labels stack up at directory.goodonyou.eco). Buy second-hand, swap with friends or even rent items – there are an increasing number of online platforms that support this, such as thredUP and Hirestreet. Most importantly, spend some time rethinking your relationship with fast fashion. Do you really need another cheap T-shirt? If the answer is yes, ask yourself why.

11. OPT OUT OF JUNK MAIL

How much junk mail do you get? Chances are it's off the doormat and into the bin so quickly that you don't even register the sheer volume of leaflets, takeaway menus and free 'newspapers' coming through your letterbox on a weekly basis – but it's a lot. Every year the average British household receives 650 pieces of junk mail,[33] adding up to 17.5 billion pieces of junk mail produced and distributed every year throughout the UK. It's annoying, and it's wasteful too.

By taking steps to prevent junk mail being delivered to your house, you'll be reducing the demand for it in the first place, which means distributors produce less, and therefore more resources – such as paper and the energy used to produce said junk mail – are saved. Of course, where there's a will, there's a way, so you're unlikely to be able to stop *all* junk mail landing on your doormat, but there are things you can do to drastically reduce how much you have to deal with.

1. If you get unwanted mail with a return address on the envelope, write 'Unsolicited mail, return to sender' on it and pop it into a post box – no stamps necessary. The sender will then have to pay for the postage and will likely remove you from their mail system.
2. Sign up to the Mailing Preference Service (MPS) at mpsonline.org.uk. This is a free service that lets you remove yourself from marketing mailing lists. It's good practice for companies to check the MPS list before sending you mail, although it's not a legal obligation. In the US, dmachoice.org operates in the

same way, with a $2 fee covering the service for 10 years.

3. In the UK, you can opt out of Royal Mail's Door to Door service. This prevents any unaddressed mail being delivered to your house (although Royal Mail is legally required to deliver all addressed mail, including items addressed 'To the occupier').
4. If you keep getting junk mail from one organisation in particular, contact them directly citing Article 21 of the General Data Protection Regulation (GDPR). Doing so means they are legally obliged to take your personal information off their mailing lists.
5. These measures won't stop local takeaways and businesses posting flyers through your door, though, so a 'No Junk Mail' sticker can be a useful deterrent. It won't always work, of course, but more reputable businesses will honour your wishes.

12. SWITCH TO A GREEN ENERGY PROVIDER

Switching your energy provider is not the faff it used to be. Thanks to the Energy Switch Guarantee, the whole process is now handled by your new supplier and the only thing you need to do is decide where you're moving to. Right now, there are more green energy options available than ever before.

As individuals, a big chunk of our carbon footprints come from the gas and electricity we use in our homes – over 40 per cent of UK emissions come from households, in fact.[34] In the past, fossil fuels were our go-to sources for powering our homes, but these resources are rapidly depleting, churn out high levels of greenhouse gas emissions and are becoming increasingly damaging to obtain. Fracking, for example, is one method of extracting oil and gas from the ground, but its risks to both people and the planet have been well documented in recent times.

Green energy, on the other hand, comes from renewable sources such as the wind, sun and sea, and has a significantly lower impact on the planet. Not only are new energy suppliers springing up to offer customers this more sustainable option, but even 'The Big Six' – once among the nation's greatest environmental offenders – are offering green energy tariffs. By choosing a green energy option, you'll be limiting your consumption of natural resources, reducing the volume of emissions released into the atmosphere and probably saving a bit of cash in the process, too.

There are plenty of comparison sites online that will help you find a green energy option. It's helpful to have the name of your current supplier and current tariff to hand, as well as a previous bill outlining your average energy consumption, but all you really need to get started is your postcode. Once you've confirmed your contract with your new supplier, they'll take care of everything, and you can flick the lights on knowing you've made a positive difference.

13. LEAVE YOUR LAWN ALONE

This is probably the easiest tip in the whole book, because it involves you doing absolutely nothing at all and making a lot of beneficial impact in the process! In short, mow your lawn less often. That's it. That's this whole section in a nutshell.

Manicured gardens and landscaped lawns might look nice, but they're no help to our friends the bees. Dandelions in particular – unfairly labelled 'weeds' by aesthetics-orientated gardeners – are a valuable food source for insects coming out of hibernation. Each dandelion head contains up to 100 individual flowers, chock-full of the nectar and pollen that bees and hoverflies need to do their job. And as far as humans are concerned, that job is to keep us alive by contributing to the world's already precarious food system through pollination. Mow over these dandelions and you're essentially throwing a bee's much-needed lunch in the bin. Other lawn plants such as clover, daisies and buttercups also act as vital pollinator pit stops.

This isn't an excuse to let your lawn become entirely wild, however, as some studies have shown that letting grass get *too* long can block insects' access to low-standing lawn flowers.[35] Ideally, your grass can be left until it's around three to four inches tall before it gets a haircut – this roughly equates to a fortnightly mow in summer, and less often in winter.

If, however, you're absolutely wedded to the idea of an immaculate garden, you might consider planting a scattering of wildflowers on a single strip of lawn and leaving it to grow freely. Not only do wildflowers require little to no tending, they look gorgeous anywhere, and pollinators love them just as much as they do lawn plants.

14. GIVE YOUR CAR THE ONCE-OVER

It's no secret that cars are bad news for the planet. Transport is responsible for nearly 30 per cent of the EU's total CO_2 emissions, 72 per cent of which comes from vehicles on the road.[36] There are greener alternatives, of course – electric vehicles are steadily gaining momentum, for example – but for some, driving a petrol or diesel car is a necessary environmental evil. So if you have to drive, you can at least make sure you're doing it as efficiently as possible, and you'll also save a bit of cash in the process.

Get into the habit of doing a few quick checks on a regular basis. The state of your tyres is a biggie. Driving on under-inflated tyres is not only dangerous, but also illegal and it means the engine has to work harder to move the vehicle, which means unnecessary emissions and unnecessary fuel costs. Plus, you'll end up spending more on tyres in the long run – a tyre underinflated by 20 per cent will give you 20 per cent less mileage before needing to be replaced.[37] Keep them properly inflated and they'll last a lot longer.

Check if you're overdue an oil change. Your car's handbook will advise you how often this should happen – it's usually every 5,000 miles or so. Dumping out the old oil and replacing it with fresh stuff might not sound very environmentally friendly, but as engine oil is essentially the lifeblood of the car, it's important to keep it clean (well, as clean as oil can be). Oil helps to prevent wear and tear on the engine, but over time it becomes more viscous, making it harder for components to move as they should. This in turn puts more strain on the engine, which, you guessed it, leads to unnecessary emissions.

Finally, have a tidy up. It's easy for your car to become a dumping ground for camping gear, kids' toys, sports equipment and so on, but if it doesn't need to be in the car, take it out. Ditto roof boxes, luggage carriers and bike racks. If you're not using it, it's just creating needless weight and air drag, which means ... well, you get it.

15. DRIVE GREENLY

While we're on the subject of cars and driving, there are a few things you can do when you're behind the wheel that'll help lessen your vehicle's impact on the environment, even if it's a gas guzzler.

Drive smoothly, accelerate gently and keep an eye on the road ahead. Harsh acceleration and braking can use up to 30 per cent more fuel,[38] not to mention cause increased wear and tear on your car. Plus, if you slow down early for traffic lights or a queue, you might not have to stop completely – rolling uses less fuel than stopping and starting again.

If you have a rev counter, aim to change gear at somewhere between 1,500 and 2,500rpm, and stick to the speed limit. Drive at 70mph and you'll use up to 9 per cent more than at 60mph and up to 15 per cent more than at 50mph. Taking it up to 80mph can use up to 25 per cent more fuel than at 70mph.[39]

When it comes to idling, there's a lot of speculation about best practice, and of course everyone reckons they know what the official advice is. The fact is, there are no hard and fast rules here – it depends on a lot of factors. According to most motoring organisations, you should turn your engine off if you expect to be stationary for more than two minutes.[40] However, older cars (eight years plus) and vehicles with older batteries (over five years) can struggle if the engine is started and stopped too often in a short space of time, plus their age means they're more likely to spurt out additional pollution every time the ignition kicks in again. As a general rule of thumb, though, you should turn the engine off if you know your car is in good nick and you'll be idling for a while, unless of course you have a car with a stop/start system, in which case this is irrelevant because it'll just decide for you.

Oh, and go easy on the air conditioning.

16. PICK UP A PIECE OF LITTER

This is an activity that really demands a bit of tolerance for your fellow man, because it essentially involves cleaning up after lazy sods whose boundless arrogance means they see fit to use the world as their trash can – so it might feel like a futile exercise. But! Picking up the odd bit of litter you come across can actually have a pretty significant impact.

For a start, litter frequently attracts wild animals, such as water birds looking for nest materials or urban foxes looking for a snack. These guys can easily choke on or get tangled up in rubbish, so taking just one piece of it off the streets could save an animal's life.

Secondly, multiple studies have linked the prevalence of litter to social challenges such as poverty and crime.[41] Ever heard of the 'broken window theory'? This idea was introduced by social scientists back in the 1980s, and states that visible signs of crime and anti-social behaviour – such as littering – lead to further instances of crime and anti-social behaviour. On the flipside, studies have shown that if an area is free from litter, it's less likely people will litter there.[42] So by picking up one piece of rubbish, you could be discouraging someone else from littering later on.

Finally, littering is just a huge waste of resources. Every time a piece of rubbish ends up in a hedge or is chucked into a river, the in-built value of that material is lost. A discarded drinks bottle won't have the chance to be made into a new one, for example. This means more resources – materials, energy, water and so on – need to be used to create another one. If that drinks bottle ends up in an actual bin, however, there's a much higher chance of it being recycled.

Plus, picking up a bit of rubbish while you're out and about will give you a nice hit of instant gratification, and you'll be a shining beacon of inspiration to your friends and family while secretly feeling pretty smug about your good efforts.

17. LEARN HOW YOUR RECYCLING SERVICE REALLY WORKS

Considering how important recycling is, you'd think the powers that be would make it as simple as possible – alas, no. There's a mind-boggling amount of variation to the process depending on where you live, with every council having its own way of doing things, and every household having different sets of bins, bags and boxes to contend with. This understandably leads to a lot of confusion – if one type of material can be recycled at your friend's place, why can't it at yours?

And this, in turn, leads to contaminated recycling, which can add up to a mountainous waste problem. Putting the wrong stuff in the wrong receptacle can mean whole lorry-loads of waste usually bound for a recycling plant instead ends up in landfill. In 2018, some 500,000 tonnes of recyclable material in the UK alone ended up going to waste because of this.[43]

Some items are pretty obvious offenders – dirty nappies, for example, regularly crop up in household recycling when they should be put in with day-to-day waste. Other items, however, are a bit more ambiguous. Plastic film, crisp packets and greasy pizza boxes will all render your recycling unrecyclable, as will food-soiled packaging such as half-eaten yoghurt in pots, butter-smeared margarine tubs and unrinsed jars and tins. And then there's 'wish-cycling', where stuff gets chucked in that – while technically recyclable – isn't collected by your particular council.

In an ideal world your council would communicate clearly exactly what it will and won't take, but here we are. To double check for yourself, pop your postcode into recyclenow.com/local-recycling to get a simple breakdown of what you can put into your recycling bins or bags. There are a few other quick and easy steps you can take, too:

1. Look at packaging labels – some items very clearly state that they're not recyclable.
2. Empty and rinse out all containers.
3. Leave lids on jars and bottles (otherwise they can get lost during the recycling process).

4. Don't forget recyclables from other rooms in the house, like bottles from the bathroom.
5. If in doubt, leave it out. Better to sacrifice one item of material to the black bin than risk contaminating a whole bag of otherwise fine recyclables.

18. DO YOUR BIT AROUND THE HOUSE

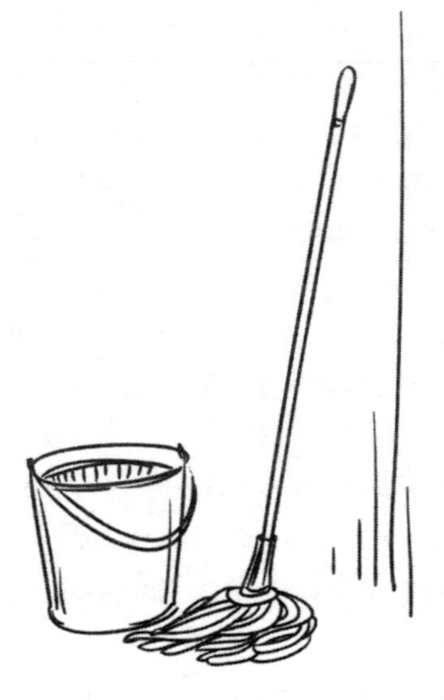

Men, this one's for you! Gender equality has come a long way since women first got the vote in the early twentieth century, but imbalances in rights, power and freedom are still rife around the world. From the gender pay gap and period poverty, to the increased threat of violence and the glass ceiling, women face a host of challenges every single day that their male counterparts do not. And in the face of all these exhausting obstacles, there remains one tedious constant responsibility that just can't be shaken: housework.

There is no end of research documenting just how much more housework women do than men. One analysis from University College London found that women do approximately 16 hours of household chores a week, compared to men's six.[44] Another, from Oxfam, says that women do on average two hours more housework every day than men (and yes, all the participants in both studies – women included – worked full-time).[45] Whatever the exact difference, it's significant, with the Office of National Statistics concluding that the unpaid labour of all women aged 18–100 in the UK is worth some £700 billion to the economy.[46]

The answer to this seems glaringly obvious: men, do your fair share around the house! But putting this fiendishly genius solution into practice, it seems, is a lot harder than it looks, thanks largely to pervasive gender norms inherited from parents or compounded by mainstream entertainment, or – in some confusion of 'progressive' male thinking – the idea that doing domestic chores somehow constitutes 'helping' and is worthy of praise.

'You should have just asked,' is the all-too-frequent reply from men who perhaps don't understand why their partner – exhausted after a day of work, making dinner and putting the kids to bed – is liable to have a meltdown upon finding the dishwasher still hasn't been emptied. But having to ask in the first place (and then again and again, until it constitutes 'nagging') is a job of work in itself – an act of management that requires mental and emotional labour.

> If keeping a tidy gaff does not come naturally to you, set a reminder on your phone, write a note on your hand or even tie a piece of string to your finger if you must. Then look around, see what needs to be done and do it without fanfare or fuss.

19. AMPLIFY MARGINALISED VOICES ON SOCIAL MEDIA

Social media is great for a lot of things, not least the brain-quieting pleasure that comes with a lost hour (or two) spent mindlessly scrolling through feeds. Who wouldn't, given half the chance, spend an entire day looking at pictures of cats and Netflix memes?

But the part of the brain that so easily gives itself over to eye-glazing 'content consumption' also means we can be pretty lazy online. We follow our friends, the brands we like, our favourite celebrities, joke accounts masquerading as live-tweeting animals and so on – all compounded by algorithms telling us who to follow based on who we already follow. So it's all just more of the same, and we wind up in an echo chamber – and given the political opinions held by some, that can be dangerous, with different groups of people living in different worlds, populated with utterly different realities.

But mitigating the potentially damaging effects of these digital media bubbles is straightforward: introduce new and diverse voices to the fold. Bring messages, causes, campaigns and different communities into your online space and share them with your followers, who can in turn share them with their followers, and so on. Spreading the messages of marginalised voices gives rise to new ways of thinking among those who may not have considered a different viewpoint before, and helps to blur the lines of polarisation that contribute to ignorance and hate, both online and IRL.

Of course, social influence is something of a numbers game and, inevitably, a popularity contest. Over on Twitter, for example, which has 145 million daily active users,[47] folk take pride in their following-to-followers ratio, and the 'blue tick' badge of accreditation lends only questionable credence to some Twitter 'personalities'.

Nonetheless, a tweet need only reach the right person to make a meaningful difference, no matter how small. So follow marginalised voices, like their posts, engage and interact. Boost their visibility with a retweet or share. Not only will that put these messages in front of people who may otherwise remain unaware of them, but it can also help point media outlets to overlooked stories and issues and, subsequently, the voices that are best placed to comment on them.

20. CALL IN PROBLEMATIC BEHAVIOUR

None of us is perfect, and against a backdrop of ever-evolving causes, movements and terminology, even the most well-intentioned activists are liable to slip up now and then. A big part of being a supportive ally, though, is correcting these mistakes, however genuine or innocuous they may be.

Enter 'call-out culture'. Calling someone out is to publicly comment on their problematic behaviour or language, and it serves two purposes. Firstly, to let the person in question know that they're being harmful, and secondly, to let *other* people know that the behaviour was harmful, thus helping to educate others while holding the original person to account.

And this all worked well enough for a while, until social media became something of an unwieldy beast and call-out culture became a toxic form of self-righteous 'performative' oppression in itself. As former US President Barack Obama said at the Obama Foundation Summit in 2019: 'If I tweet or hashtag about how you didn't do something right, or used the wrong word or verb, then I can sit back and feel pretty good about myself, because, "Man, you see how woke I was. I called you out." That's not activism.'

But since staying silent about injustice often means being complicit in oppression, problematic behaviour still needs to be addressed. This is where calling *in* is effective, particularly if the person in question is a friend or family member who you know deep down means well. Calling in involves having a private, personal conversation with an individual without making a spectacle of it. It's considered a less reactionary way to work through conflict, and recognises that people are multifaceted, and that a mistaken instance of oppressive behaviour or language does not necessarily define who we are. Calling in is not a straight-up alternative to calling out, though – the latter still plays an important role in activism, particularly in cases where the individual (or brand, business, organisation, etc.) *should* know better, or continues to exhibit harmful behaviour despite constant call ins.

One very important note, though: for those on the receiving end of oppressive behaviour, constantly calling in is an exhausting form of emotional labour. As such, it's up to allies to do it when and wherever they can.

IF YOU
HAVE AN
HOUR . . .

1. CALCULATE YOUR CARBON FOOTPRINT

'Carbon footprint' – a term once the sole preserve of climate scientists – is now a household phrase. In a nutshell, it's the measure of impact that human activities have on the environment in terms of the amount of greenhouse gases we produce, measured in units of carbon dioxide (CO_2). We've all got an individual carbon footprint (unless, of course, your entire lifestyle involves living naked in a field, unsheltered and surviving only on thin air – and even then you'd still be producing a minuscule amount of carbon). The way we use everything, from petrol and electricity to clothes and food, contributes to our carbon footprint, directly or indirectly.

The size of the average person's annual carbon footprint varies wildly across the world. Globally, the average is 4.7 tonnes, but it's probably no surprise to learn that those in Western countries have considerably larger carbon footprints than those in less economically developed regions. According to Oxfam, the average person in Rwanda, for example, has an annual carbon footprint of 0.09 tonnes. In the UK, however, the average is a significantly higher 8.3 tonnes.[48] Or, to put it another way, it would take the average Brit just *five days* to create the amount of emissions someone in Rwanda does in a *year*.

Now, if we're going to limit rising global temperatures to 1.5°C – which scientists agree will prevent the worst consequences of climate change (see page 149 in the glossary) – we need to cut CO_2 emissions by 80 per cent by 2050, which means that in an ideal world we'd all be living a 3-tonne lifestyle. For those in the West, that's a fairly lofty goal, but again, if we *all* took steps to reduce our carbon footprint then getting the global average down to 3 tonnes is far more feasible (this doesn't take into account the enormous carbon footprints of business and industry, though – again, that's another book).

But you can't work on reducing something if you don't know what it is you're starting with, so taking the time to calculate your personal footprint is a great jumping-off point for reducing your individual impact. There are dozens of carbon calculators available online. The WWF (World Wide Fund for Nature) has a straightforward, easy-to-use questionnaire that reveals lots of interesting climate-related facts and titbits as you progress. Conservation.org, meanwhile, lets you calculate the carbon footprint of individuals, families, trips and even events. There's also carbonindependent.org, which offers a much more in-depth, statistics-driven calculator that really digs down into the carbon-based nitty gritty of your lifestyle. Whichever calculator you use, revisit it regularly – once or twice a year – to keep on top of the differences your actions are making.

2. GET YOUR BOILER SERVICED

Boilers are good sports, really. They go largely ignored for long periods of the year, and then as soon as the first chilly winds of autumn set in, we're all over them like an old high-school friend trying to sell you off-brand cosmetics on Facebook. And as the old saying goes, if it ain't broke, don't fix it, so as long as your radiators are heating up and there's enough hot water for a shower, it's easy to just let it get on with things.

But like any other bit of complicated engineering, a boiler really needs an annual service to keep it in tip-top condition. For a start, regular checks help to keep you safe. Carbon monoxide poisoning comes with a host of symptoms (dizziness and nausea, for example) that are often mistaken for other common illnesses, and some 4,000 people in the UK end up in A&E every year because of it.[49] Regular services help to mitigate this risk.

An annual service will also help you save money in the long run. Firstly, you'll be able to identify small issues before they become major (and expensive) problems, and regular maintenance will help reduce the need for repairs in the future, so your boiler will last longer. Secondly, a regular service will make sure your boiler is running as efficiently as possible. Over time, tubes and pipes get clogged up and parts wear down, which means you have to use a whole lot of extra fuel in order to achieve the toasty warm results that you're used to. This means higher heating bills (and we already spend about 60 per cent of our yearly energy costs on heating)[50] and a big waste of energy and emissions.

Of course, your boiler won't last forever even if it is regularly maintained. When it's time to make the switch, opt for the highest efficiency-rated boiler that you can. An A-rated boiler could save you hundreds on your energy bills and make the payback period – the length of time it takes for a boiler to 'pay for itself' in savings – much shorter.

A side note for tenants: you might not have much jurisdiction over the boiler in your property, but it's the law in the UK for landlords to organise annual safety checks for all gas appliances in their properties – and this includes boilers.

3. DRAUGHT-PROOF YOUR HOME

Draughts are public enemy number one when it comes to keeping your home warm and cosy. All that lovely heat whooshing through cracks and crevices means you have to use more energy to achieve the same result, which is bad news for your carbon impact and your wallet, since you're literally paying to heat the outdoors.

But draught-proofing is easy, and it's one of the cheapest and most effective ways of saving energy in the home – or any type of building, for that matter. According to the Energy Saving Trust, draught-proofing around windows and doors will save you around £20 a year on your energy bills, while draught-proofing a chimney that's not being used will save around £15 a year.[51] Not only that, but draught-free houses are more comfortable at lower temperatures, so you might be able to turn the thermostat down a notch or two, which would save you even more dollar.

Obviously, you could pay someone to come and do it for you, but DIY draught-proofing is pretty failsafe. First off, you'll need to identify draughty areas, so spend some time feeling around windows, doors, loft hatches, floorboards, plug fittings, skirting boards and chimneys. If the air is cooler here, you've got a draught.

Your standard DIY store will have everything you need to tackle the problem. Foam strips are useful for doors and windows, while flexible fillers and sealants will take care of draughts around floorboards and pipework. Chimney balloons, meanwhile, are super easy to install yourself. A letterbox flap brush and keyhole cover will also make the world of difference to a draughty front door.

If you're a tenant, you're within your rights to ask your landlord to address these issues on your behalf, but since these changes don't constitute significant remodelling or redecoration – and actually increase the appeal of the property – you can usually just go ahead and sort it yourself. Just be careful not to block up any intentional ventilation, such as extractor fans, underfloor grilles and airbricks, wall vents and trickle vents (which are usually found above modern windows) – these are important for keeping your house fresh and dry.

4. GET A SMART METER

Smart meters may seem like a relatively recent addition to our domestic set-ups, but the technology behind them has actually been kicking about since the 1970s[52] – it's only with the widespread adoption of home broadband and government energy-saving initiatives that they've really come into the spotlight.

For the uninitiated, a smart meter is a palm-sized device that sits in your house and measures how much energy you're using at any given point. It also sends meter readings directly to your energy supplier, and gives you all kinds of data on the way you're using power and how much you're spending. The UK government has been on a crusade to get one into every home and small business in recent times, and as such, most energy companies offer them (and their installation) for free to their customers.

An energy meter in itself won't save you any money or reduce your energy consumption, but it gives you the information you need to make changes that will. Once installed, you can see in real time how much power your home is using, and the immediate tangible difference that comes with turning lights on or boiling the kettle – and that's a powerful behavioural driver. In the intro to this book we looked at the importance of being able to *see* the results of our actions, and smart meters capture this well, albeit on a micro level.

One study by Smart Energy GB suggests that 85 per cent of households in the UK have made positive changes to their behaviour thanks to their smart meter, and that customers can expect to save on average £250 on their bills over a period of 20 years (for the very energy-hungry among us, that could be much more).[53] Granted, this isn't an earth-shattering sum, but again, it's collective behaviour that makes a difference. Come 2024, smart meters in the UK are projected to have saved the nation around £5.6 billion and slashed emissions by 45 million tonnes[54] – that's enough to power nearly 5.2 million homes for a year.[55]

Most suppliers are already encouraging their customers to adopt a smart meter, and if they're not yet then they will be soon, thanks to government targets. Installation is straightforward, having a smart meter won't impact your ability to switch providers and in many cases it'll give you a wider choice of (cheaper) tariffs, too. Plus, it's quite fun to run around the house turning things on and off and seeing what makes the biggest change to the numbers.

5. CHANGE YOUR LIGHT BULBS

The incandescent light bulbs of yesteryear are long gone now, having been phased out by the UK government in 2011. As they gradually disappeared from the shelves, we all made the dutiful switch to compact fluorescent lamp (CFL) bulbs, halogens and, in a few cases, LEDs, and energy-saving light bulbs became the norm (the situation is less clear-cut in the US, however, where incandescent bulbs are still available alongside their newer counterparts).

But the gripping world of domestic lighting is constantly innovating, and a lot of folk don't realise that things have changed quite considerably since the departure of incandescents. For example, a limited range of CFLs and some halogens were the go-to for dimmer switches, since LEDs weren't compatible with these types of fittings, but both could take a while to warm up, and while LEDs lit up quickly, they were generally cold, harsh and ultra-bright, and absolutely not conducive to cosy mood lighting.

Now, though, LEDs reign supreme. They're dimmable, come in a wide range of fittings and sizes, work as spotlights and, crucially, produce a lovely spectrum of lighting styles, from eye-wateringly bright whites to soft, warm and inviting hues. They're also the most efficient type of bulb available – the Energy Saving Trust says that replacing all the bulbs in an average home will save about £40 a year on bills.[56]

LED bulbs are generally more expensive than CFLs and more efficient halogens, but they last for ages. With a lifespan of around 35,000 hours, an LED will last two to four times longer than a CFL and up to 35 times longer than an old-school incandescent.[57] This means that the bulb pays for not only itself over and over again in the long run, but that you'll be producing considerably less waste and pollution, since light bulbs involve a hefty amount of manufacturing, transportation, energy production and disposal.

Of course, if the bulbs in your home are already energy-efficient and are working fine, there's no need to add to the world's growing waste problem by unnecessarily buying replacements. But when the time comes, opting for LEDs is definitely a *bright* idea (sorry!).

6. REQUEST SOME FREE WATER-SAVING GADGETS

If you live in the UK or a particularly wet state in the US, you'd be forgiven for thinking that an abundant supply of rain means things are okay water-wise. Alas, no. While climate change is responsible for more extreme weather events such as storms and flooding, it's also responsible for increasingly long periods of drought-like conditions and heatwaves (which are dangerous to humans and animals alike), and water companies capture much less rain than people commonly assume.

In the UK, for example, more than half of water companies operating in England are rated as being under serious water stress, and the demand for water – which is around 140 litres per person per day – is only set to rise in the coming years.[58] It's not only important that we ensure a sustainable supply of water for everyone in the future, but conserving water where we can also minimises the volume of additional resources being taken out of rivers, which has a negative impact on wildlife and vital ecosystems.

There are lots of obvious things you can do to help conserve water: take shorter showers, collect and reuse rainwater in the garden, turn the taps off when you brush your teeth, and so on. But these all require an element of effort. The good news is that with a few water-saving gadgets, you can drastically reduce your water consumption without having to give it any thought at all. And often, these devices are free from your water company.

A Water Hippo, for example, is essentially a plastic box that sits neatly in your toilet cistern and saves up to 3 litres of water per flush by keeping hold of water that would otherwise be needlessly flushed away. One of these can save enough water to make up to 35,000 cups of tea a year![59] Tap inserts, meanwhile, help to reduce water flow from household taps from 10 litres per minute to just 5, and because they cause the water to aerate, you won't notice any difference in pressure.

Water companies are keen to conserve water, so many will give these types of gadgets to their customers for free (or for a vastly discounted price). Visit water.org.uk to find your water supplier in the UK, or inmyarea.com/utilities in the US, then check out your supplier's website to see what they can offer you.

7. MAKE A MEAT-FREE DINNER

Even though they're on the rise, vegetarianism and veganism remain somewhat divisive lifestyle choices. Proponents of plant-based diets are often more than willing to wax lyrical about the many benefits of their lifestyles, much to the chagrin of devout carnivores for whom a meal without meat is simply unthinkable. But cultural clashes aside, there's no doubt that meat – and the way we consume it globally – is bad news for the planet.

Livestock production creates more greenhouse gases than the entire transportation sector – and that's not just down to flatulent cows. It drives deforestation, takes up the vast majority of farmland and hoovers up an enormous volume of resources – producing just one quarter-pound beef burger uses around 1,695 litres of water, for example.[60] In fact, researchers have consistently demonstrated that the single biggest way to reduce your environmental impact on the climate is to cut meat from your diet.[61]

But that's a pretty big ask for some people, and this book is all about making manageable changes, so instead of trudging resentfully into a meat-free existence (although you should definitely consider it if you can), you can still make a pretty significant difference by simply reducing your meat consumption. A study by Greenpeace, for example, recommends no more than 460g of red meat per person per week – that's about the equivalent of three burgers.[62] If everyone did this, meat consumption in the EU would drop by approximately 71 per cent by 2030, helping to mitigate farming's contribution to climate breakdown.

Or try committing to one meat-free day a week, à la the 'Meatless Monday' campaign spearheaded by Paul and Stella McCartney back in 2009. Skipping just one serving of beef a week for a year saves the equivalent emissions of driving 348 miles in a car[63] – if everyone in the US did this, it would be the equivalent of taking 7.6 million cars off the road.[64]

Of course, there are no end of vegetarian recipes available online to provide some meat-free inspo, but for those who just can't get enough of the taste of meat, plant-based dupes have come a long, long way since the early days of pulverised mushroom. The likes of the Impossible Burger and Beyond Meat – which have even grabbed the attention of traditional meat-dealing giants like Burger King – are doing an increasingly popular trade in extremely convincing alternatives.

8. LEARN A RECIPE FOR SCRAPS AND LEFTOVERS

Considering food is so critical for our survival, we sure do waste a lot of it. Over a third of all food produced globally ends up in the bin, and when you take into account the energy, water, labour and agricultural processes used to make this food, it adds up to $1 trillion in wasted value.[65] More disheartening still is the fact that the world's one billion hungry people could be fed on less than a *quarter* of the food that is wasted in the US, UK and Europe.[66]

'Stop wasting food' is the obvious takeaway here, but that's easier said than done. Picky kids, hectic social lives and a proliferation of cheap and tempting food delivery options makes buying the right amount of food, and using it before it spoils, something of a challenge. Even the most ardent meal planner lacks the psychic ability to know with certainty how their week is going to pan out.

But learning one or two simple recipes can help you make a dent in the world's growing food waste mountain – you just need to be aware of what it is you're wasting. If you go through a lot of potatoes, for example, try sautéing the leftover skins to make a delicious crispy snack. If that forgotten bunch of bananas is rapidly turning brown (and don't worry, we all start the week with good five-a-day intentions), mash them up and turn them into a cake.

If you have a couple of favourite go-to meals that always leave you with some awkward leftover ingredients – half a can of tuna or a bit of swede – try a new dish that will make use of them. Lovefoodhatewaste.com/recipes is a brilliant resource – just search for the leftovers you've got and it'll give you a huge range of recipe options that can be filtered by cooking time, dietary requirements and difficulty.

9. PLANT A TREE

There are a lot of reasons to be grateful for trees – they suck up carbon, produce oxygen, stabilise the soil and provide homes for all kinds of wildlife. And really, what's more idyllic than sitting beneath a great shady tree on a summer's day, listening to the gentle breeze rustle through its branches, or stomping through big piles of brightly coloured crispy leaves come autumn?

The good news is that the planet is looking a lot greener than it used to. Since 1982, an area covering 2.24 million square kilometres – roughly the combined land surface of

Texas and Alaska, two of the biggest US states – has been added to global tree cover.[67] In the UK alone, the Woodland Trust has planted more than 47 million trees since the early 1970s.[68]

The problem is, it's still not enough to help mitigate the harmful effects of climate change, and the UK comes up woefully short against its European neighbours – just 13 per cent of the UK's total land area has tree cover, compared to an EU average of 35 per cent.[69] Add to that the ever-present issue of global deforestation, which clocks in at a loss of around one football field of forest every *single second*,[70] and things don't look so rosy.

There are plenty of government initiatives in place around the world to address this shortage of trees – suffice it to say, some are more effective than others, and some are merely thinly veiled attempts at greenwashing – but action on a collective level has a really tangible benefit here.

There are multiple variables to factor in when you're considering the numbers around tree planting and carbon offsetting – a lot depends on the type of tree, where it's planted, the rainfall it gets and so on. In 2019, though, a physicist for tech and science publication *Wired* estimated that if everyone on the planet planted a tree, it could eventually reduce global dioxide levels by around 6 per cent.[71] That's not an enormous figure, but every little helps in the fight to keep global warming below 1.5°C. Plus, planting a tree comes with lots of individual benefits, too, such as improved property values and lower energy bills thanks to shade and shielding, not to mention the physical and mental benefits that come with living near greenery.

And planting a tree is really, really easy. Providing you have the space to do it and pick the right type for your climate, all you need is a young tree (which can cost as little as £10/$20) and a hole in the ground. If you don't have a garden, you can still get involved. Check out tree-council.org for community tree-planting initiatives in the UK, or onetreeplanted.org for projects in the US.

As well as making a positive difference to the climate, you'll also have the joy of watching something beautiful and delicate grow big and strong, knowing that you're the reason for its existence. Sort of like having a kid, but with less mess.

10. MAKE YOUR GARDEN BIRD-FRIENDLY

Wonky street pigeons and furious dive-bombing seagulls aside, the presence of birds is a great indicator of the health of our natural surroundings. The healthier the environment, the more likely birds are to make it their home, and while a spot of relaxed garden birdwatching is good for the soul, it's important for the wider ecosystem, too. Birds help to control pests, pollinate plants and spread seeds, all of which help plants and trees survive and thrive, which is critical in our fight against climate change.

According to the RSPB (Royal Society for the Protection of Birds), however, garden bird populations in the UK are on the decline.[72] The reasons for this are still being investigated, but fewer green spaces, pollution and a changing climate are just some of the challenges faced by our feathery friends. But there are simple things you can do to help them out.

Firstly, give them a tasty treat. Food is the main reason birds will come to your garden, so serve up snacks all year round with a bird feeder filled with premixed bird seed or a simple mix of sunflower seeds, hemp and oats. Keep this off the ground and near to cover if possible – this helps them keep an eye out for potential predators such as cats and squirrels.

Next up, make sure there's clean water on offer for drinking and bathing. A proper bird bath or small water feature is ideal (birds seem to be attracted to gently moving water), but they'll splash around in anything, really – an old washing-up tub or even a bin lid will do the trick. In the winter, pop a cork or ping pong ball in to help stop the water from freezing over.

Finally, give 'em some digs. Birds are industrious wee things and they're quite capable of seeking shelter and building a nest when they need to, but we all know how tedious house hunting is, so you can make things easier for them by installing a nesting box if you've got the space. Put them in sheltered spots away from direct sunlight (and away from other boxes, as birds are notoriously territorial) and let them get on with it – you don't need to put anything inside; they'll take care of that themselves. All you need to do is give them a clean once a year during the autumn – just make sure no one is home first.

11. GET TO KNOW YOUR NEIGHBOURS

That seminal Australian soap opera had it right: everyone really does need good neighbours. Things like keeping the noise down, bringing the bins in on time and respecting allocated parking are all guaranteed to make everyone's lives easier and more pleasant, but there's a wealth of evidence to show that actually getting to know your neighbours has massive benefits for the wider community.

Not only is knowing your neighbours practical and useful (you've got someone to call on if you need a package signed for or if your car needs a jump-start, for example), but it also pays dividends from a mental and emotional perspective. Did you know that some nine million people in the UK say they are always or often lonely, although two-thirds say they'd feel uncomfortable admitting it?[73] Of the 1.4 million chronically lonely older people in the UK, around half a million will go more than five days straight without seeing or speaking to another person,[74] while one in four new mums say they're lonely 'often or always'.[75] Meanwhile, the charity Sense says that 50 per cent of disabled people experience loneliness on any given day.[76]

It's a dangerous epidemic, with studies estimating that loneliness can increase the risk of premature death by around 30 per cent,[77] so small actions here can make a big difference. Of course, it might feel a bit weird to suddenly wedge yourself into someone's life – especially if you've already been neighbours for a while – so start small. A simple 'hello' over the garden fence helps to get a relationship off the ground and opens up lines of communication for the future.

Alternatively, pop a note through the door introducing yourself and giving a number to call in case they need anything. Some people, especially older folk, might not be keen on asking for help, so you could list some of the things you might do for them, such as shopping, posting letters or doing odd jobs around the house like changing light bulbs or taking out the rubbish. You don't need to make a point of their age or circumstances – just be neighbourly!

You could also introduce yourself with some food ('Oh, I made too many cupcakes and wondered if you'd like some') or with a greetings card during a holiday or faith-based celebration. During periods of bad weather, such as cold snaps and heatwaves, you might knock on the door with a cheerful 'Cor, what about this weather?' and an offer to help, should they need anything. Once you've established a bit of a relationship, you're in a good position to check in periodically, whether it's for a cup of tea or just a simple status check. Don't overdo the unscheduled visits, though – no one likes a *nosy* neighbour.

12. JOIN A LOCAL SWAP-AND-SHARE GROUP – OR START ONE!

Back in 2015, the phrase 'sharing economy' was added to the Oxford English Dictionary for the first time – proof that the term, first coined in 2008, was here to stay. Since then, the definition has fractured somewhat and is often used interchangeably with all kinds of buzzwords, such as 'collaborative consumption', 'peer economy' or 'on-demand economy' – many of which refer to slightly different economic principles or techy start-ups, such as Uber and Airbnb. The fact is, though, that the 'sharing economy' as a concept has existed for as long as man has walked the earth. Simply put, it involves sharing your underused stuff with other people.

It's not only neighbourly, but it's good for the planet. When was the last time you used your electric drill or that stepladder sitting in the shed? Both of these items have an inherent value in terms of the energy, materials and resources used to create them, but that value is essentially wasted every time someone else goes out to needlessly purchase the same thing – and then double the waste eventually ends up in landfill. Letting someone else use or even have your thing instead of them having to buy their *own* thing mitigates this.

Of course, not all of us have the type of relationship with our neighbours that facilitates the casual borrowing of stuff, hence the creation of platforms such as Freecycle and Freegle. According to Freecycle, its nine million members are keeping more than 1,000 tonnes of stuff out of landfill every day,[78] while the UK-centric Freegle says its service has yielded an economic benefit of more than £3 million over the 12 months up to August 2020.[79]

Both organisations function within a community context, but more mainstream social media sites are also acting as member-organised swap-and-share platforms. Facebook and neighbourhood-based social network Nextdoor, for example, are home to hyper-local groups that connect those who need something with those who have it, and vice versa.

The chances are you have a few items lying around that you don't use all the time. Power tools are a common request, as is gardening equipment and temporary party and event furniture, such as folding chairs and trestle tables. By listing them on one of these sites – which really only takes a matter of minutes – you could help save a neighbour some money *and* prevent the unnecessary use of valuable resources and eventual waste associated with them buying that item new. And if *you* need something, it pays to check out these platforms before parting with your cash. No group local to you? Start your own! You definitely won't be the only person in your area with stuff to share.

13. VISIT A CHARITY SHOP

There used to be a lot of snobbery around charity shops, and to be fair, many of them were once indeed synonymous with dusty shelves strewn with questionable bric-a-brac and bulging rails of musty, misshapen clothing. But no longer! Charity shops have seen a major reputational overhaul in recent times, thanks largely to an increased narrative around sustainable fashion (see pages 28–9) and dire economic times catalysing all-round thriftiness.

Charity shops are now an integral part of the high street, and a boom in 'boutique-style' charity shops – plus untold headlines about savvy buyers unearthing amazing designer finds for basically pennies – means they are now very much a go-to for those looking for a unique bargain.

But there are plenty of other reasons why a visit to a

charity shop is worth your time beyond finding a great deal. Charity shops help to divert hundreds of thousands of tonnes of textiles away from landfill. They raise more than £295 million every year for a range of causes,[80] as well as invaluable awareness for campaigns and specific charities, and the sector provides more than 24,000 local, stable jobs in the UK, plus more than 234,000 volunteering opportunities.[81]

These volunteering opportunities are particularly important for those looking to boost their employability skills, and for combatting social isolation and loneliness among older volunteers. In fact, Community Service Volunteers estimates that for every £1 spent on volunteer programmes, some £3.38 of social value is created, including improved mental and physical health within local communities.[82]

But these benefits can only be realised if charity shops continue to be supported, both through shoppers making purchases and with individuals donating their unwanted items. Fortunately, the profile of charity shops is only set to increase, with research suggesting almost one in three people believe the importance of charity shops has grown following the COVID-19 crisis, and almost a fifth of people aged 25–34 saying they will be more likely to visit charity shops than before.[83] Still not convinced? Pay a charity shop a visit on your next lunch break – you might be pleasantly surprised!

14. SWITCH UP YOUR SANITARY CARE

Contrary to the punchy tampon adverts showing women bouncing merrily around tennis courts in white skirts during their time of the month, periods are generally a miserable business. At this point in your life, though, you probably know what works best for you and your body, and this book is not about to lecture you into changing that. Menstrual cups, for example, are getting a lot of attention these days, and while they tout a number of environmental benefits, they're definitely not for everyone, so you'll find no guilt trip here.

However (yes, sorry), it's no secret that regular tampons and sanitary towels are kind of problematic from a waste standpoint. The average woman in the UK will use between 11,000 and 16,000 sanitary items in her lifetime,[84] and as there's no way that material can be repurposed or recycled, it all ends up in landfill (or, if it's flushed down the loo, in sewers and waterways). Without making the switch to a menstrual cup or increasingly popular 'period pants' (super-absorbent underwear that lets you free-bleed without leaks), a lot of this waste is unavoidable. But! Simply switching up your brand can make a positive difference.

Tampons with plastic applicators are some of the biggest environmental offenders, so consider switching to those with cardboard applicators – sustainable tampon brand

TOTM makes tampons with biodegradable applicators, for example, each wrapped in recyclable paper. Or invest in a reusable applicator, such as the one made by DAME, which works with every size of tampon and is completely carbon neutral.

Pads, meanwhile, are also responsible for their fair share of plastic waste. According to organic sanitary brand Natracare, the average pack of conventional pads contains up to five carrier bags' worth of plastic.[85] However, Natracare's alternatives – as well as others on the market – are completely plastic-free and made from natural, breathable materials.

You might even give reusable sanitary towels a go – they've come a long way in recent times and can offer the same level of protection as their disposable counterparts. In fact, according to reusable sanitary towel brand Bloom & Nora, their colourful reusable pads perform *better* than disposables, and customers claim they're more comfortable than the sticky variety.[86] If you've ever had an errant adhesive strip stuck to your nether regions, you'll know that's a pretty strong selling point.

15. GIVE YOUR FINANCES AN ETHICAL OVERHAUL

Banks and building societies aren't just places to stash your cash – they're responsible for driving the world's economy, so it follows that they have a sizeable impact on what actually happens in the world. Predictably, some are more well intentioned than others, and so unless you're hiding your cash under the mattress (and who could blame you, really?), making the switch away from the bad guys to more ethical financial institutions can send a strong message to those at the top.

All of the world's major banks have made commitments to sustainable practices in some shape or form, but much of the time these efforts are merely thinly veiled attempts at greenwashing. HSBC, for example, has pledged to spend $100 billion on sustainable investments by 2025,[87] yet it remains one of Europe's top fossil fuel financiers.[88] Barclays, meanwhile, holds an annual 'Green Finance Conference' and offers a range of so-called sustainable products such as loans and investments, but it's also spent more than $85 billion on fossil fuels,[89] making it the sixth-largest funder globally. In fact, according to the Rainforest Action Network, 35 of the world's biggest banks funnelled $2.7 *trillion* into fossil fuels between 2016 and 2020.[90]

So, what can you, a lowly current account holder with a modest overdraft, do? In a word: move. Switch to a more ethically minded bank, such as The Co-operative, Triodos or Ecology, all of which ensure that no part of their business funds damaging activities such as fracking or deforestation, while investing instead in socially and environmentally beneficial projects and ventures.

While these banks are lesser known, they still offer all the usual savings, loans and investment products you'd find at a 'traditional' bank, and they're still covered by the Financial Services Compensation Scheme (so up to £85,000 of your money is protected should they, like any other bank, go bust). Furthermore, these banks tend to offer better interest rates than their high-street counterparts.

Making the switch to a new bank is easy thanks to the Current Account Switch Guarantee (see currentaccount switch.co.uk), and it's set to become a popular choice – the UK market for socially responsible investing is expected to grow by 173 per cent to reach £48 billion by 2027.[91] Of course, this is where collective action comes into play again. One person making the move towards more ethical banking is a drop in the economic ocean, but *everyone* doing it would create a ripple of accountability for financial institutions in the face of these increasingly critical global issues.

16. READ UP ON SOCIAL ISSUES

If you're reading this book, you're probably a decent enough person. You're likely reasonably clued-up on the world's ills and realise that while there has been some progress within movements calling for social equality among marginalised groups, there's still a lot of work to be done. And much of it comes down to intention.

It's not enough to be non-racist, non-sexist, non-homophobic. The tireless efforts of activists before us have helped pave the way for the *non*. Now, it's time to be anti. Anti-racist, anti-sexist, anti-homophobic. Movements don't need well-meaning bandwagon-jumpers posting supportive hashtags and taking part in essentially meaningless social media 'challenges', all the while hoping quietly for better days (although as discussed in the introduction, raising awareness is still an important element). What they need are supportive communities to inform, educate and commit to change.

But, as noted earlier, relying on those from marginalised groups to constantly show and tell you how to do this puts the exhausting burden of enacting change on them (when they already have enough to deal with). As an ally, you need to take the initiative, and educate yourself. How? Read. Read the news – from trusted news sites and not just Twitter. Read the stories of those whose lives are affected by intolerance. Read the novels and non-fiction of women, people of colour and LGBTQ+ folk, and spend time reflecting on their experiences. Read about the history of oppression and arm yourself with the facts – the real facts, not the questionable stats from a meme shared by your aunt on Facebook.

Knowledge is power – the power to enact meaningful change. Understanding the deeper nature of these issues and educating yourself on their far-reaching impact means you're in a stronger position of allyship. You've got the bedrock to call out (or *in*, see pages 47–8) friends and family for their damaging comments, to make decisions about where you spend your money and how you use your civil rights.

Most importantly, reading up on these issues can help you confront your own challenging thought processes. Everyone wants to think of themselves as a reasonable, tolerant individual, so it can be uncomfortable to find that you yourself have – albeit unknowingly – subscribed to problematic thoughts and behaviour. But facing this head-on is vital. Back in the Nineties and mid-Noughties, for example, it was the cultural norm to use the term 'gay' as an expression of displeasure. You can guarantee that many of those who did this had no intolerance of, or ill will towards, the LGBTQ+ community, but they just didn't realise the damaging impact this behaviour had. Then people got educated, and things started to change. So keep things changing by getting educated.

17. START A NARRATIVE AT WORK

The way we work is changing. As the millennial cohort increasingly dominate the workforce, jobs are no longer about simply clocking in and clocking out – this generation of workers (and Gen Z coming up behind) expect that the companies they work for think of society and environment alongside profit, and make a meaningful contribution to the world. In fact, three-quarters of 18–34-year-olds say they expect their employer to take a stand on important issues facing their country and constitutional rights.[92] Meanwhile, LinkedIn says that 86 per cent of millennials would consider taking a pay cut to work for an organisation whose values are aligned to their own – a figure that stands in stark contrast to the 9 per cent of baby boomers who would do the same.[93] It's also heartening that some 70 per cent of millennial workers believe that employees can make an even greater impact on the world than the leaders who run organisations.[94]

So it's no surprise that employee activism is on the rise,[95] and this can take many forms. High-profile cases involving corporate giants like Amazon and Google are well documented, with walk-outs, protests and press junkets doing an important job of shining the accountability spotlight on companies that are, frankly, getting away with a lot. But it can also take much smaller, simpler forms that have a beneficial knock-on effect beyond the workplace.

Implementing a recycling initiative at the office, for example – paper in one bin, other materials in another – will make a modest difference to that particular organisation's environmental impact, but the engagement necessary to get it started, such as team meetings, memos and regular reminders, helps to instil a behaviour that can be replicated at home, too.

All parties stand to benefit. Enabling employee activism has consistently been shown to prove critical to a business's longevity, from boosting productivity[96] to reducing staff turnover,[97] not to mention an enhanced reputation and lots of ticks in those CSR boxes. These are the desirable companies that people *want* to work for, so it's in every business's best interests to foster a culture that inspires employees to give back and to engage with issues that matter to them.

So what's the takeaway here? Start a conversation with your colleagues and bosses. Ask what your company could be doing better. Are there any local issues where the organisation could make a difference? What about fundraising initiatives? Are there opportunities for volunteering? Even something as seemingly inconsequential as an office-wide drive to ensure teabags are put in the right bin can make a difference and start a chain reaction that can drive further activism in both the workplace and at home.

18. PRACTISE ACTIVE LISTENING

Mobile phones, email, social media ... technology might have made communication easier, but that's come at a price. We might hear what others are saying when they speak, but are we really *listening*? Genuine listening involves time, and we're definitely low on that these days.

And according to Edgar Dale's 'Cone of Experience' theory,[98] we only remember 25–50 per cent of what we hear, which means we're missing out on a lot of potentially important information from those around us.

Enter 'active listening', a style of listening that keeps you engaged with your conversational partner in a positive way. This is where you make a conscious effort to hear not only the words that another person is saying, but, more importantly, the complete message being communicated. Successful active listening helps to build relationships, ensure understanding and resolve conflict. It helps to earn trust, and makes people feel valued, supported and less alone – these are particularly important endeavours when it comes to allyship. Being an active listener means you recognise that the conversation is more about your partner than about you.

And it's more challenging than it seems. Active listening, unlike passive listening, which is really just hearing, is *work* – it's not something that just happens. It requires conscious effort and an intentional push back against some of the sloppier conversational habits a lot of us are used to. But it's a skill worth mastering, because in these times it's more important than ever before that people feel heard. Some tips:

1. Use physical cues to show your partner you're giving them your full attention. Face them, make frequent eye contact and give the odd gesture of encouragement, such as a head nod or verbal 'uh-huh'. Don't fiddle with anything, and definitely don't have one eye on the TV or your phone.
2. Don't interrupt. Tempting as it might be to respond with an example of your own experience on the topic at hand, keep the conversation focused on your partner. Ask open-ended questions, if appropriate, to encourage them to keep talking.
3. Shut down your internal dialogue. This can be tricky, as most of us are always subconsciously running through our to-do lists or thinking about what to have for dinner. Instead, try to visualise what's being said, in pictures – this is an effective memory recall tool, plus it helps to encourage genuine empathy.
4. Be patient. Sit with periods of silence and let the speaker take their time – don't rush them along.
5. Defer judgement. Listen without jumping to conclusions and without judging the other person, or mentally criticising them. If what they say makes you feel alarmed, go ahead and feel alarmed, but then push it to one side so you can refocus your attention on your partner.

6. Paraphrase. Repeating back what the other person has said is a great way to clarify information and to reassure them that you're truly listening. 'What I'm hearing is ...' and 'It sounds like you're saying ...' are good ways to reflect.
7. Words only convey a fraction of the message, so watch out for non-verbal cues, too.

19. LOBBY YOUR LOCAL MP OR MEMBER OF CONGRESS

There are a lot of things we as individuals can do to make the world a bit of a better place, but there will always be times when we come up against a bunch of legislation that puts the brakes on meaningful action – and that's where your local officially elected representative can help.

Members of Parliament (MPs) – or, if you're in the US, members of Congress – are theoretically there to do one job, and that is to serve you, the constituent. They've been elected to represent your interests, and despite the many turning cogs in the political machine, they *can* help to influence government policy. Doorstep recycling collection in the UK, for example, was the direct result of people coming together to lobby their MPs for change.[99]

Writing letters and emails, attending local town hall events and visiting your representative during their open office hours (called 'surgeries' in the UK) are all important ways of highlighting causes and campaigns that could benefit from their backing and subsequent political clout. Many of them have decent social media platforms, which can help spread that all-important awareness of an issue, and of course many of them will welcome the opportunity to get some positive public face time under their belts.

Not every MP or member of Congress will be receptive to your efforts, though, which can be pretty disheartening when you feel like you're already under the boot of bureaucracy. So it pays to research your rep's background. In the UK, theyworkforyou.com is a great site that tells you all about your local MP, their political party and their voting record, while house.gov/representatives is a similar US-based resource. Using these, you'll be able to get an idea of what your representative is about and their particular political focus, and from that determine how best to engage them.

Some top tips for lobbying your local rep:

1. Do your research, both on your representative and the issue you're raising. Be prepared with a bank of resources, examples and statistics relating to your cause.
2. Know what you want to say, and what you want to achieve. Communicate this clearly and concisely to

your rep, whether by letter/email or at a meeting in person.

3. Follow up! If you don't receive a response to your letter or email, send another. If your rep agrees to take direct action on something but appears to be dragging their heels, follow it up. If something changes that affects your cause – perhaps new research is released, for example – make sure your MP is aware of it by, you guessed it, following it up.

There's a fine line between gentle and consistent pressure and stalkerish harassment, of course, so do remember that these people are reasonably busy and can't give their undivided attention to any one constituent or issue. Work on establishing a good relationship with your MP or member of Congress and your cause is likely to move higher up their agenda.

20. USE YOUR VOTE (AND ENCOURAGE OTHERS TO DO THE SAME)

Voting is probably one of the most important civil rights that we as individuals have – and it's the defining example of collective activity in action. Voting gives us the opportunity to support the political candidates whose views and beliefs mirror our own, and who are well placed to enact the changes we want to see in the world.

Now, the frameworks in place in both the UK and US mean that it's far from a perfect system. 'First past the post' versus proportional representation, and the popular vote versus the Electoral College, mean that major political voting events see their fair share of controversy. This, amid the deafening noise of campaigning, media spin doctors, mud-slinging and divisions that lead to fall-outs with family and friends, means it's no surprise that a lot of people choose to just ... not. Engaging with the politics and current affairs around an election can be confusing and exhausting, so some folk opt out of the process altogether.

That's their right, of course (except in places like Australia, where a failure to vote comes with a penalty), but it's repeatedly been demonstrated that it's this cohort that has the most power to influence voting outcomes. During the UK's 2017 General Election, for example, some 13.63 million people voted for the Conservative Party, while the Labour Party secured 12.88 million – they missed out on the majority by just 750,000 votes. Non-voters, meanwhile, accounted for *14.5 million* lost votes.[100] Then, of course, there's the now-historical EU Referendum in the UK in 2016, which closed at a razor-thin 51.9 per cent to 48.1 per cent majority in favour of Leave – some 72.2 per cent of the UK's eligible voters turned out to vote that day,[101] but what would have happened if the other 27.8 per cent had shown up? Or even just 2 per cent of them? The UK's political landscape could look wildly different now. And let's not forget the 2020 Presidential Election in the US, where Democratic candidate Joe Biden managed to swing a number of traditionally Republican states by a knife-edge margin.

'Voting doesn't make a difference anyway' is the popular narrative from apolitical types explaining their (lack of) action, but it is quite simply not the case. Political parties write policies to benefit their supporters, and the more supporters they have from a specific demographic, the more likely they are to pay attention to the wants and needs of that group. As mentioned during the introduction to this book, one wasp at a picnic is no big deal, but a swarm is a game changer. You have to be part of the swarm if you want to change the game.

IF YOU
HAVE A
DAY...

1. HAVE A SPRING CLEAN

Unless you're a devout follower of Mrs Hinch, the prospect of a day spent cleaning probably isn't the most appealing proposition, but it's worth it for a number of reasons. Firstly, there's nothing quite as satisfying as curling up on the sofa at the end of the day knowing your gaff is squeaky clean and spotless, and secondly, it could actually reduce your carbon footprint – and energy bills – in the long run.

Take your oven, for example. If it's covered in grease and grime (and again, no judgement here), then it has to work harder to reach the correct temperature. If it's clean, it'll reach the right temperature more quickly, helping to conserve energy. It'll also distribute heat more evenly, which means more evenly cooked roasties and springier cakes.

Have you looked behind your fridge lately? It might not be a pretty sight with dust and grease slowly building up on refrigerator coils. This forces the fridge to work harder to keep things cold, so spend a few minutes giving them a wipe down. And while you're at it, have a sort through the inside of the fridge, too. Rotting produce and items past their use-by date are just taking up valuable real estate – keeping your fridge around two-thirds full will help it run most efficiently.

Other cleaning hotspots include lamps and light bulbs – keeping them cobweb-free helps them run at maximum capacity – and around radiators. If you've got double-panel radiators you might be surprised (horrified) to discover the amount of dust and fluff fermenting in there. And again, this means that you have to crank up the thermostat even higher to achieve the room temperature you're after, and that's just a waste of energy and money.

Finally, giving your windows a quick clean can improve the amount of natural light in your home, which could mean you don't have to rely on electric lights quite as much. Cleaning the filters in your washing machine and tumble dryer will help these appliances run more efficiently, too.

2. GET RID OF YOUR UNUSED STUFF

As a nation we sure do have a lot of stuff. And not just items we use every day, like phones and kettles, or even things used less frequently, such as hiking boots and toastie makers, but all the bits and pieces strewn around attics and sheds, packed away in boxes under beds and shoved in corners, never used and gathering dust. *Stuff*. In fact, according to research from eBay, the average UK household is sitting on 42 unused items, worth around £2,600.[102]

And this stuff is taking up valuable space in your house and on the planet. One study, for example, suggests that household product consumption is responsible for up to 60 per cent of global greenhouse gas emissions.[103] And when those products are shoved in the attic and forgotten about, that's a big waste of resources.

But as discussed earlier, there's almost certainly someone out there that's after whatever it is that's dominating your storage space – one man's trash is another man's treasure, after all. So it's worth spending an afternoon rounding up all your unused junk and getting it into the hands of someone who will actually use it – you might even make a bit of spare cash.

Swap-and-share groups (see pages 74–6) are a good place to start, especially if you're willing to let your stuff go for free. Then there's the likes of eBay, Gumtree and Freecycle, as well as dedicated platforms geared towards offloading specific items – Music Magpie for games and music, Depop for clothes, and so on. And of course charity shops (see pages 76–7) will always be grateful for donations.

But there's something else this book has not yet covered – a wondrously retro British institution of an activity that can yield all kinds of surprises: the car boot sale. Pitch up in a field in the middle of nowhere, fling open the boot of your car and be instantly inundated with bargain hunters, lurking around like vultures and getting in your way before you've even unpacked the trestle table.

Car boots can be a lot of fun if you go in with the right attitude. You're not going to make bank, but you will get a bit of friendly chit-chat, cash for a few pints later on and a day of fresh air. Plus, someone will be happy to have taken your unwanted stuff off your hands, and you'll be going home to a less cluttered house.

3. INSULATE YOUR LOFT

One for the homeowners, this, unless you have a particularly considerate and proactive landlord (in which case, *never move*). As much as a quarter of a home's heat is lost through the roof of an uninsulated house, so taking action here can have a major pay-off, both in reducing heating bills and slashing carbon emissions.

Decent loft insulation will last for around 40 years and will pay for itself multiple times over – and in most cases you can even do it yourself. There are plenty of DIY tutorials online, and insulation material itself has advanced a lot in recent times, meaning it's much easier to handle than the fiddly flaky stuff of yore.

According to the Energy Saving Trust, insulating the loft of a detached house will cost around £395, so it's not the cheapest thing you can do to help the environment.[104] However, that will knock around £215 off your energy bills every year, so it will pay for itself in under two years. It'll also stop around 950kg of CO_2 from entering the atmosphere, which is the same amount emitted by a car driven for 2,323 miles.[105]

Of course, few among us have the luxury of a detached pad, but the savings involved in insulating a mid-terraced house are equally decent. Expect it to cost around £285, but you'll save £135 a year in bills – that's a payback period of just over two years. This will also prevent the emission of 550kg of CO_2, which is equivalent to the emissions generated by charging 70,143 smartphones![106]

Reducing emissions is a central focus of the UK government's environmental agenda (largely because it's bound by ambitious international targets), so it's worth checking to see if there are any active financial incentives or grants available to help with energy-efficiency improvements. In 2020, for example, the government launched the Green Homes Grant, which gave householders in England up to £10,000 for energy-efficiency measures. Keep a lookout for more initiatives like this in the future. The same applies if you're in the US, as many areas offer public utilities grants to help cover the costs of energy-efficiency enhancements.

4. PLANT A VEGETABLE GARDEN

... or patch, box, tub, pot – whatever you have room for. The last few years have seen a big rise in the number of folk growing their own veggies, and that's a trend that's set to continue.[107] Of course, being able to smugly show off your lovingly nurtured tomatoes or spuds on Instagram has a major appeal, but as the increasingly fragile food system takes more prominence on the global stage, people are waking up to the many other benefits of home-grown produce. It comes with a lower carbon footprint, it's good for the bees (see also page 34) and it does away with all the unnecessary packaging waste that dominates supermarket shelves. Plus, it's good for you – not only does home-grown produce taste amazing, but there are plenty of studies that show a spot of green-fingered activity can help combat stress and anxiety.[108]

Growing your own veg can seem like a daunting prospect, though, especially if you're the type that struggles to keep a regular houseplant alive (guilty), so start small. Plants like tomatoes, beetroots and runner beans are easy to care for and will generally do their own thing without too much intervention. Or you could start with a simple herb garden. Check out the Royal Horticultural Society's website (rhs.org.uk) for loads of failsafe advice and info.

No garden? No problem. According to Wyevale Garden Centres, some 66 per cent of people grow plants in their kitchens.[109] Lots of veggies will grow quite happily in pots or baskets on a windowsill – tomatoes, peppers and spring onions are quite content indoors, for example. And if you're keen to really dive in but don't have the space, you could consider applying for a plot on a local allotment. These are usually pretty sought-after, though, so you might see if there's a local community gardening group near you instead – that way you'll also get lots of tips from seasoned pros.

5. VOLUNTEER YOUR TIME

It's a tired and cheesy notion but it holds true: in this hectic world the greatest gift you can give someone is your time, because none of us has enough of it, really. Making room in your schedule for volunteering is one of the most powerful things you can do to enact meaningful change in your community.

People have a lot of preconceptions about volunteering; that it requires unwavering commitment to a rigid schedule, that you need some kind of experience in a certain field or that you'll end up having to do all the gross jobs. And this might be true in some cases. But volunteering is generally pretty flexible and is definitely hugely diverse. Whether you've got the occasional hour to spare or can set aside a whole day or afternoon on a regular basis, there are countless opportunities to get involved in good causes in ways that reflect your lifestyle, values and priorities. And volunteering takes all kinds of forms, from helping with administrative work and fundraising, to providing transportation or simple companionship. And yes, there are plenty of chances to get your hands dirty, if you want to.

The impact that volunteering has on society is significant. The economic value of volunteering has been estimated at £23.9 billion in the UK alone,[110] with many causes and organisations dependent on volunteers to stay afloat. Without them, they wouldn't be able to continue their vital and often life-changing work.

But it's not an entirely selfless endeavour – volunteers get a lot out of it, too. New skills, improved employment prospects, the chance to meet new people and pursue an interest outside of work, and so on ... volunteering can be really enjoyable. Plus, knowing that you're making a difference for a cause you believe in and helping to empower others is a pretty big win for your self-esteem. Visit do-it.org (UK) or volunteermatch.org (US) to find an opportunity that works for you, or ask your employer about workplace volunteering days.

6. TAKE PART IN A SPONSORED ACTIVITY

If you log on to Facebook right now, the chances are your news feed will feature at least one or two well-meaning pleas for money. Your old housemate is walking 100 miles for a medical research charity, John in accounts is giving up booze for a month ... that sort of thing. And it's tempting to give these folk a customary 'like' and scroll on past, but as tedious as it might be to hear about Marie's seasonal cycling event or whatever, sponsored activities like these are a good way to raise awareness of causes close to individual hearts, as well as a bit of cash for the charities that support them.

You *could* fling a fiver in the direction of every person who asks for sponsorship for their activity, or you could just *be* that person and commit to your own endeavour (although obviously, if you've got the cash, do both). Whether it's an officially organised activity, like a fun run or marathon (oof), or an individual undertaking like shaving your head or giving up chocolate (also oof), making a public commitment to doing something makes it a central focus of your life for a while. And in turn, that'll give it – and its associated cause – greater prominence in the lives of your friends, family and whoever has the dubious honour of following you on social media at that time. And as noted at the start of this book and countless times since, it's that awareness that's important.

But as already mentioned, there are lots of fundraisers and lots of causes out there vying for attention, so your efforts need to stick out. Play to your strengths and weaknesses. No one will be particularly enthused about sponsoring an outdoors-loving rock-climber to hike up a mountain, for example. There's no challenge involved, plus people will probably already be bored of hearing them wax lyrical about hills at any other given time. But if that rock-climber announces he'll have his chest waxed before the event as long as a certain amount of money is raised, people are more likely to pay attention.

Also, keep people updated with your progress and preparation. It's not enough to bombard friends and family with requests for money – let them see that you're working hard towards a goal and take the time to give something back, whether that's through regular updates or cute video messages thanking people for their support. Finally, if you work for a large organisation, it's *always* worth asking if they offer match funding or any other support for fundraising activities by employees – many do.

7. BECOME A BLOOD OR BONE MARROW DONOR

The human body is a pretty spectacular thing, with millions of processes happening every single second to keep us alive and well. But despite this extraordinary machinery, we're all still ultimately soft flesh bags with a species-wide tendency to accidentally damage ourselves. And of course, sometimes the machine malfunctions and we get sick.

Thanks to modern medicine, though, many of the potentially life-threatening risks associated with illness and injury can be mitigated by sharing our bodily wealth. Or, more specifically, blood. The average adult has around 10 pints of blood in their body, which for most people is more than is needed at any one time. Offload just one pint as a blood donation and you could help save up to three lives.[111]

Around 830,000 people give blood every year in England alone, but services across the whole of the UK always need new donors – according to the NHS, around 400 new donors are needed *every day* to meet demand.[112] Giving blood is a quick and painless procedure that simply involves having a nice lie-down and then scoffing some biscuits afterwards. The websites blood.co.uk in the UK or redcrossblood.org in the US are good places to search for donation facilities near your location.

Or, if you're already a blood donor and want to up the ante a bit, you might consider registering as a bone marrow donor. Bone marrow is the soft, spongy tissue found in the centre of certain bones that produces blood stem cells. People with blood diseases such as leukaemia, lymphoma or myeloma often need a stem-cell transplant, and in about 30 per cent of cases, a donor can be found from within a patient's family. The remaining 70 per cent of the time, though, patients have to rely on a volunteer donor.

In the initial stages of registering you won't actually donate anything. Instead, a few painless cheek swabs are taken, and your stem-cell information will be uploaded onto a 'matchmaking' database. There are more than 17,000 known bone marrow characteristics, resulting in millions of combinations, so finding a matching donor is not unlike finding a needle in a haystack – as such, you can see the significance of coming up trumps. The British Bone Marrow Registry (bbmr.co.uk) or bethematch.org (US) both contain loads of information on how you could save a life this way.

8. SPEND TIME WITH YOUNGER PEOPLE

'Children are the future' is a pretty clichéd phrase, and in the grand scheme of things it's easy to lose sight of the meaning behind it – time marches on, kids become adults and still the world faces its fair share of problems. But right now we're at an important crossroads, where thanks to the internet and social media young people are more informed and more connected to one another than ever before. And the results are notable – look at Greta Thunberg, who mobilised kids all over the world to take part in historic climate strikes, or the young Parkland students, whose protest movement following a mass shooting at their high school in February 2018 helped catalyse a series of gun control measures in the US.

Their efforts also helped to spark a historic surge in youth voter turnout in the midterm elections.

If these kids are the future, then we've got a lot of reasons to be hopeful. But not all young people are coming to adulthood in an environment of activism and positive change. Some – too many – are growing up facing significant challenges, from poverty and crime to a lack of education and other forms of oppression. And all of this informs a worldview that follows them into adulthood, which goes on to shape the world.

Having a positive role model can make a massive difference to the life of a young person. Countless studies show that kids having someone decent to look up to makes them more likely to finish school, less likely to start using illegal drugs or become involved in criminal behaviour, and more likely to have higher self-esteem.[113] Could you be that person?

Parents and primary caregivers obviously have a major role to play in their kids' lives, but anyone who's ever been young will tell you that your parents are the least cool people on earth when you're a teenager. This is why these positive role models usually take the form of a coach or teacher, family friend or other relative. So if you know a younger person, spend some time with them. Talk about the stuff that matters to them, share your experiences and practise active listening (see pages 86–9) – just be the person you'd have wanted around when you were their age. If every young person grew up feeling heard, valued and supported, the future could indeed be a much rosier place.

9. EDUCATE YOURSELF ABOUT YOUR FAMILY HISTORY

There are a lot of unanswered questions in life, and when significant stuff happens – good or bad – it's not uncommon to find yourself pondering the bigger picture. Why are we here? What's the meaning of life? What happens when we die? You know, that cheery sort of thing.

And while we can't ever know the answers to these questions, we can help to fortify ourselves for future musings by trying to understand our own pasts – and it's a really pivotal time to do so. Our digital world means our generation is the first to have a readily accessible online archive of every single moment of our lives, from seemingly insignificant pancake disasters and Friday work beers, to major life events such as falling in love or having kids. But this wasn't the case for our parents and grandparents, and so the only way we'll ever know about their lives – and by extension, our own heritage – is by asking them. There's definitely a creeping sense of urgency about this. When these relatives go, their stories will go with them.

Genealogy websites have seen an explosion of activity in recent times. Ancestry.com, for example, handles more than one billion searches every month,[114] while many sites have also expanded to offer DNA testing that promises to tell you all about your genetic inheritance. But neither of these resources can paint a colourful picture of your family history. Records are often incomplete or come with challenges such as surname variations or fudged dates. DNA sites, meanwhile, can't tell you anything about your culture. Culture comes from lived experience, traditions and stories passed down from actual people who mould our perceptions of the world.

So take some time to talk to your relatives. Ask them the questions that explain the events that shaped them, that led to the decisions they made and the lessons they learned. The answers, whether joyous, dull, exciting or bleak, can give us important new insights on life, as well as a greater sense of compassion and understanding, both for the many hundreds of lives that eventually led to ours and for those we're surrounded by now. It's human nature to crave a sense of belonging and shared experience, and we all feel stronger if our single threads are woven into a tapestry.

10. TAKE A FIRST-AID COURSE

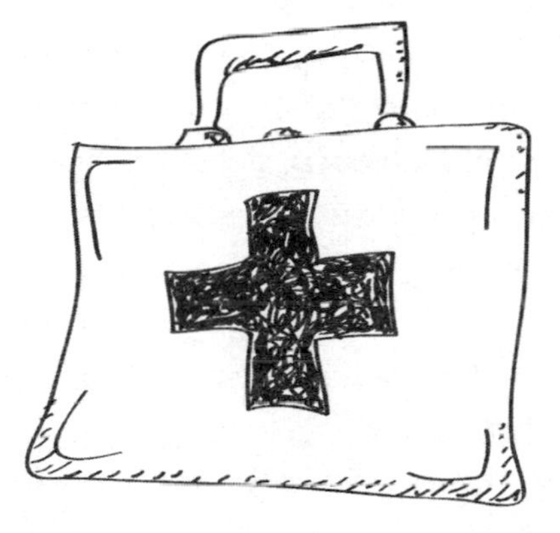

Most of us know what to do if someone grazes their knee or accidentally scalds a finger in the kitchen, but what if something more severe happens? In situations where someone's health is seriously at risk, administering first aid promptly and effectively can mean the difference between life and death.

And yet, according to the Red Cross, just 5 per cent of adults say they'd feel confident enough to provide first aid in an emergency situation. In cases where the emergency services are called, first aid is only attempted around half the time before medical help arrives, despite there being someone at the scene 96 per cent of the time. As such, the Red Cross estimates that some 59 per cent of deaths from injury could be prevented if first aid was administered before the emergency services took over.[115] That's a lot.

First aid isn't just about saving lives, though (although that is obviously the main objective). Being able to properly administer first aid from the moment of an incident (or as soon as possible afterwards) can help reduce a patient's pain and discomfort in what is usually a very stressful situation. Plus, it can help their recovery time, reduce their time spent in hospital and reduce pressure on already-squeezed health services. Knowing that your actions can have this impact is pretty empowering.

It's frankly baffling that first aid isn't compulsory in schools, but until it is there are plenty of ways you can get trained up. First of all, it's always worth asking your employer if there's a workplace first-aid training programme in place. If not, search for courses near you through the British Red Cross or St John Ambulance in the UK, or the National Safety Council in the US. They'll be able to direct you to comprehensive local courses that will equip you for all kinds of medical emergencies. Many offer group training options, too, so get your mates to come along – after all, you need them looking out for you as well!

11. LEARN A NEW SKILL

You know those times when you're chatting to someone at a party and they casually mention a particular hobby or interest, and you think, 'Wow, that's cool, I'd love to try that!' Well, what's stopping you? Learning new skills doesn't have to end in school or college, nor does it have to be synonymous with tedious training days at work.

Take a class, watch an online tutorial, buy a guidebook or just have a bash at your own pace – there are plenty of ways to get to grips with a new skill in whatever way you feel most comfortable. And the pay-off goes beyond the skill itself. Learning new stuff keeps your brain agile and helps you adapt to change – studies even show that learning new skills helps to stave off dementia.[116] It gives you the opportunity to meet new people, it's satisfying and, ultimately, it's fun (unless it's not, in which case that particular pursuit might not be for you).

Getting skilled-up is also a great way to enhance your everyday activism. A lot of the more sought-after skills among folk who 'wish they were good at that' include things like sewing, gardening and DIY – all of which can have a direct impact on the planet. Learning to sew means you can repair clothes instead of buying new ones (see also pages 27–9), while gardening could lead you to growing your own veg (see pages 102–4), so you'd no longer need to buy over-packaged air-freighted stuff from the supermarket. Or, you could use your new skill to get creative for causes that are close to your heart – turn pottery into vases celebrating body positivity, or dance into performance pieces highlighting social injustices.

Learning new skills doesn't have to be a *worthy* pursuit, though. Anything that makes you happier and more fulfilled is reason enough to explore them – the world definitely needs more happy and fulfilled people. And if nothing else, it'll give you something interesting to talk about at parties!

12. VISIT AN ART GALLERY OR HERITAGE SITE

Whether you live in a city packed with chic, glass-walled art galleries, a smaller town with an oddball niche museum or out in the sticks near a natural heritage site, chances are you've got some kind of cultural hotspot within visiting distance.

These places do more than give us the opportunity for a great day out. They help build social capital and preserve customs and culture. They act as important community hubs, and help foster connections between people, businesses and organisations. They provide important jobs and opportunities for volunteering (see pages 104–5), and they help inject money into local economies. One report, for example, suggests that for every £1 spent by visitors at a city-centre museum, £12 is spent elsewhere in the local area.[117]

These places enrich our understanding of the world around us and encourage us to make positive changes to our lives. They're springboards of creativity and inspiration for kids and adults alike, and they can provide welcome respite from our troubled world. Taking in the awe-inspiring surroundings of Stonehenge or gazing upon the great works of Frida Kahlo, for example, can be a great antidote to the stress of car trouble or a tedious work issue.

The problem is, we tend to take these places for granted. Because so many of these sites are basically on our door-step it's easy to adopt an 'I'll get around to visiting them one day' mentality. But they need continual support. Staff wages, utilities overheads, maintenance, marketing, conservation, security, legal fees ... these places aren't cheap to run, and even those that charge entry fees rarely break even and are reliant on grants and private funding to stay afloat.

So what can you do to help keep these wonderful places going? Visit them! Drop a few coins into the donations box (if you can spare them), tell your friends about your trip and share snaps on social media (if you're allowed to take photos, of course). Buy a postcard in the gift shop or have a cup of tea in the café. And if there's a particular museum that you're really into, consider becoming a member or taking up membership with an organisation that looks after lots of sites, such as English Heritage, the National Trust or Cadw in the UK. You'll be making an important contribution to the longevity of these places, and you'll usually score some freebies or member perks, too.

13. GAIN SOME PERSPECTIVE FROM THE GREAT OUTDOORS

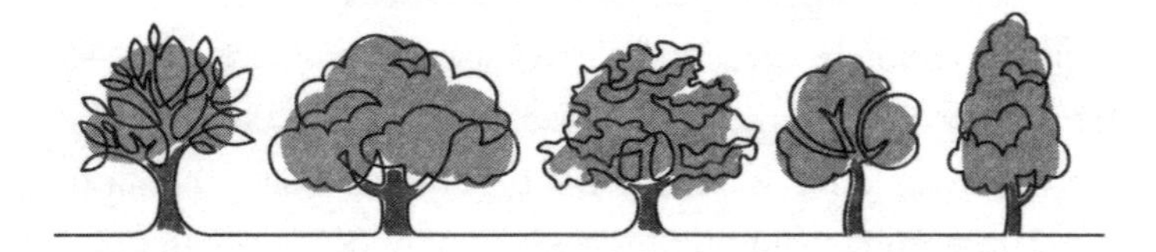

Okay, so most of us don't live near 'the great outdoors' in the traditional sense – we're more likely to have a council-managed green space on our doorstep than a sweeping mountain range or majestic lake. But it's still important to get outside and spend some time in nature, whatever form that might take.

For a start, there's piles upon piles of evidence that shows being outside is good for our health. That's not really a huge surprise, given that most of us spend our days hunched over a computer in a stuffy, poorly lit room listening to co-workers bang on about their dull weekends. A few hours in the fresh air surrounded by a bit of greenery has been shown to reap all kinds of physical benefits, from boosted immunity[118] and better sleep,[119] to better cognitive function[120] and even improved vision.[121] And then there's all the feel-good mental health wins, such as higher levels of happiness,[122] lower stress[123] and improved creativity,[124] among others.

So yeah, nature is definitely good for you. But just as taking a bit of time out to smell the roses can be a powerful antidote to the ick of modern life, it also provides a great opportunity to peacefully reflect on your place in the world, as well as life 'in the grand scheme of things'. Spending time among plants and decades-old trees that continue growing merrily regardless of what's going on in the news is a very calming, even humbling experience, enabling you to more clearly focus on what's really important to you, and therefore where best to direct your energies in life.

Plus, of course, being among nature is the best way to remind ourselves that the planet is precious and needs looking after. We all know we should be diligently recycling and using our cars less often and so on, but when you're surrounded by all that beautiful natural stuff it really hits home just how important those kinds of actions are.

14. TAKE PART IN A BEACH CLEAN

While we're on the subject of nature ... Around eight million pieces of plastic pollution find their way into the world's oceans every day, adding to the more than five *trillion* bits of trash already floating around.[125] And nowhere is safe – plastic can be found on every beach in the world, from tourist hotspots to uninhabited tropical paradises. Scientists have even recently discovered microplastics embedded deep in the Arctic ice.

It's everywhere, and not only is it gross to look at, it's seriously bad news for marine wildlife. Every year more than one million sea birds and 100,000 marine mammals and turtles are killed by plastic pollution, and scientists reckon that by 2050 every single sea-bird species on the planet will be eating plastic on a daily basis.[126] It won't be long until we're joining them, either, as around one in three fish caught for human consumption is caught with plastic in its system.[127]

Given the scale of the problem, there's no easy fix, but through that good ol' collective action, we can make a difference. First of all, the obvious one: stop littering (see also pages 38–9). While it's certainly the case that a lot of beach trash comes from illegal dumping practices, most of the stuff you find – bottles, plastic bags, cigarette butts and food wrappers – comes from the general public. Secondly, take part in a beach clean. There are plenty of officially organised beach-clean events you can join, or you can just head out on your own armed with a bin bag and a pair of gloves.

No, you're not going to be able to get rid of all the litter from all the world's seas, and yes, the chances are that even if you get one stretch of beach looking completely spotless, the next high tide will just bring in a new carpet of garbage. But it's still absolutely worth doing. Even if you pick up just two or three bits of rubbish, that's two or three fewer items of plastic in the ocean that pose a threat to wildlife and which eventually break down into equally dangerous microplastics. If you take part in an organised event, meanwhile, you'll usually be asked to record your findings, and this provides valuable data for scientists and researchers working on the bigger picture.

And of course, there's that awareness again. Talking to people about your beach-cleaning activities and sharing pictures on social media of the trash you collect gets people thinking about the wider issue of plastic and how they consume it. And this in turn puts pressure on manufacturers to take responsibility for their role in the issue. Coca-Cola, PepsiCo and Nestlé are behind the majority of plastic bottles found on beaches worldwide, for example. Thanks to lobbying by marine groups and conservation organisations, these companies have all pledged to take steps to minimise the impact of their products on our precious ocean ecosystems.[128]

15. ATTEND A PUBLIC TALK OR LECTURE

Granted, the term 'lecture' isn't particularly inviting and probably conjures up flashbacks of difficult university modules or getting a telling-off from your parents, but public lectures – let's call them talks – are a great way to broaden your understanding of the world and get to grips with topics you might not have considered before.

Public talks range from massive auditorium-filling events featuring celebrity experts, to smaller community gatherings with local specialists. They're designed to be as intellectually accessible as possible, so they're suitable for everyone, and they cover a huge range of themes. If you can think of a topic, chances are there's someone out there giving a public talk on it – the baffling variety of TED Talks available online is proof of this.

Of course, there are plenty of fascinating talks available to view on the internet, but if you're able to, attending a talk in person is a much more enriching experience. It's a low-key way of meeting new people and making valuable connections, for example. You'll also usually have the opportunity to ask the speaker questions or debate other audience members (if you want to), which can help refine your understanding of a topic or get a deeper insight into someone else's knowledge and lived experience. It's also pretty inspirational to be in a room full of engaged, curious and like-minded folk, and that sense of belonging can help to reinforce your desire to see positive change in the world.

Eventbrite is usually a good place to start exploring what's on offer in your area, as are local university websites, libraries and art centres – you'll probably also find more popular talks through Facebook's ever-omnipotent Events algorithm. Of course, it's tempting to choose talks about topics you're already familiar with, and there's nothing wrong with that – you want to have a decent time, after all. But going to a talk outside your usual comfort zone can be like a breath of fresh air for a tired brain, inspiring fresh thinking and encouraging you to draw connections between things you might not have considered before. In any case, it's always fun to learn something new, and you never know when it might prove useful in a pub quiz.

16. SUPPORT A LOCAL EVENT

It's Saturday morning (or afternoon, depending on the night before), and you're thinking about what to do with your day. What does your usual list of ideas look like? Shopping? Cinema? Gym? Sofa until it's time for the pub? All absolutely fine and standard weekend endeavours, but next time you're at a loose end, you might consider popping along to a local community event.

These take all kinds of forms: art shows, coffee mornings, charity gigs, food festivals, pop-up markets, indie film screenings … and you'll usually find them advertised in your local listings rag or, predictably, on Facebook. They might not necessarily be your cup of tea, but there are lots of good reasons to go along and show your face for at least a bit.

Firstly, it's super easy to take these sorts of events for granted: 'I'd like to do this, but I can't really be arsed today, so maybe I'll pop along next time.' If everyone said this, though, there wouldn't be a next time. Local events need footfall to be viable, and if they bomb once, they're unlikely to be repeated.

Secondly, they're really good for the local economy. As well as helping to raise the profile of an area and (hopefully) drawing in visitors and their cash, these sorts of events rely a lot on locally sourced services: food, music, entertainment, photography and so on. This benefits the businesses of local people – more on this on pages 16–18. They're also good for boosting community spirit, helping neighbours get to know one another and encouraging a sense of pride in their local area.

And they can be surprisingly fun. Don't underestimate the hilarious bafflement of a harvest festival's vegetable sculpture competition, for example, or the adorable chaos of a village dog show. And if nothing else, they can make for some good #content (which comes with its own social benefits – see pages 45–7). So the next time Facebook flashes up a poetry slam or bake sale based on the activity of your mum's cousin's friend's step-daughter, or whatever, it's definitely worth giving it another look.

17. JOIN A COMMUNITY ACTION GROUP

Where we live is more than the four walls we call home – the communities around us play an integral part in our wellbeing and happiness. Being part of a safe, thriving neighbourhood gives us a sense of belonging and fulfilment that we take with us into the wider world, and strong communities that work together are well placed to enact positive changes that also spread further afield.

Community action groups take all kinds of forms. There are residents' associations, for example, that come together to give their neighbourhood a greater voice than members would have individually. This holds a lot of sway when it comes to things like campaigning for better local services or encouraging authorities to take action on a specific issue.

There are community action groups that go by that very title: community action. These groups often mobilise with a common goal in mind, such as improving the environment of a specific neighbourhood, or fighting social issues such as homelessness or food poverty. Then there's the eminent Neighbourhood Watch, which brings people together to tackle crime and anti-social behaviour in their local area.

Regardless of the exact name or terminology, these groups provide a great opportunity to make a meaningful difference in your area, and they really do make an impact.

Studies show that Neighbourhood Watch groups can help to reduce crime by as much as 26 per cent.[129] Community action champion Groundwork, meanwhile, has rafts of evidence to demonstrate that communities working together can significantly improve local environments,[130] while wellbeing movement Action for Happiness has shown that neighbourhood networks play a vital role in both the mental and physical wellbeing of their residents.[131]

Taking part in a neighbourhood litter pick or keeping an eye out for shady activity on your street isn't going to change the whole world, but it could make a difference to *your* whole world, or the worlds of your neighbours. And in any case, global change always starts on a local level, so what better place to start than on your own doorstep?

18. ATTEND A PROTEST OR RALLY

We're living in something of a golden age of protests right now. History books are full of examples of people taking to the streets to voice their dissatisfaction, but never before have we seen so many sustained protests in so many geographical areas in such a short period of time.

Of course, smartphones and social media are playing a big role in this. Once upon a time it would take months, if not years, for a movement to gain enough traction to mobilise en masse. The historic March on Washington in 1963, for example, was born of nearly a decade's worth of activism and planning. Now, we can move far more quickly, with protests organised and numbers recruited in a matter of days.

And in many ways, this has changed the effectiveness of protests. Compared to the norm-shattering events led by the likes of the Suffragettes or striking miners, modern-day protests are a bit more two-a-penny and often lack the gravitas seen in historical demonstrations of resistance. But that doesn't mean protests don't work. Of course, the ultimate objective is change, but authorities and lawmakers are generally unlikely to bow to singular instances of public pressure. The effectiveness of protests now demands a more long-term view.

Movements are influential because over time they change the minds of people – including those who may not actively take part in them. Protests are a part of this; a grab for attention that pushes wider conversations about the cause in question and creates that all-important awareness. For individuals, protests help to validate beliefs and encourage a sense of community, which in itself is powerful. And in many cases, attending a protest can turn the casual participant into a lifelong activist, which has its own impact on society.

But most importantly, protests work in the long term because they challenge one of the most critical elements of authority: legitimacy – and a society without legitimate governance doesn't function well, thus catalysing change.

Consider this. The Black Lives Matter movement has seen significant activity in recent times, even though its roots date back to 2012. In 2016, some 40 per cent of Americans reported supporting the movement[132] – by 2020, that figure had risen to 66 per cent.[133] The movement – of which protests form a critical part – is slowly galvanising a shift in the accepted way of thinking about things.

Protests are often seen as immediate explosions of discontent and resistance, designed to enact instant change. But really, their strength lies in repeatedly focusing action over a sustained period, bringing more like-minded people into the fold and showing those in charge that the cause is not going away. So grab a placard and make some noise.

19. MAKE THE MOST OF YOUR CONNECTIONS

'It's not what you know, it's who you know' is another well-worn expression, used traditionally to describe getting your foot in the door for a job interview or nailing a deal at work. And while this kind of nepotism is increasingly being pushed aside in favour of people actually knowing their stuff (not completely, though – looking at you, politicians), it still holds true for a lot of situations, including activism.

And we all know a lot of people. It's a baffling figure, but researchers estimate that the average person knows more than *600* other people in some shape or form.[134] Obviously not all of them are going to be folk you'd invite to the pub, or even people you'd wish a happy birthday on Facebook, but they're people on your radar nonetheless, and they've all (probably) got something to bring to the table.

Say your friend has just started working at a vegetarian café – you also sort of know someone who writes a food blog. Tell your blogger connection about this cool restaurant and maybe they'll visit and write about it. Other folk will visit, and maybe one or two will decide that vegetarian food isn't all that bad and make a concerted effort to reduce the amount of meat they eat.

Or perhaps you know a budding photographer – you might let them know about a protest a friend of a friend is organising. They go along, take some amazing shots and they get shared on social media, helping to bring attention to the protest's message. Or you hear that someone wants to put on a community storytelling night and remember that your bar-manager friend has a hireable space in their venue. And so on and so on.

In all of these instances – and the zillions of potential others – your connections and proactivity have made positive things happen. There are a lot of people in your orbit

– think about what they could do for each other if they had someone to bring them together.

20. LOOK AFTER YOURSELF

'Self-care' is a bit of a tedious buzzword right now, but scrape away all the associated fluffiness of sheet masks and long baths and its central ethos is pretty simple: look after yourself. For people attuned to the problems of the world and who strive to make a meaningful difference, this is really important.

Activism fatigue is a very real thing, regardless of where you fall on the spectrum of involvement. Whether you're marching at demos every weekend or fighting the good fight online, a constant awareness of the scale of the problems we all face can leave you feeling knackered, burned out and fed up. And no matter how deeply you subscribe to the idea of collective action as a force for good, it's not unusual for your efforts to sometimes feel a bit ... pointless.

But activism in its many forms is a marathon, not a sprint, so it's important that you take time for yourself to make sure you can go the distance. There's a reason why airplane safety instructions tell you to put your own oxygen mask on first: once you've got your own mask on, you're in a better position to help those around you.

Exactly what shape this self-care takes is deeply personal. For some it may well be an hour in a hot bath with some fancy skincare or spending the evening writing a gratitude journal. For others, it might simply be making sure you're getting enough sleep and eating right or catching up on your Netflix shows. It's hard to recognise your own needs when you're focused on the needs of the world, so finding what works best for you is a process in itself.

Talk to friends about the way you feel. You don't have to be 'on' 24/7 – it's okay to admit that sometimes you just can't be arsed with it all any more. Give yourself a break from the news and be kind to yourself. Allow yourself to make mistakes and grow from them. And remember, you can never control the outcome of your activism – you can only control whether or not you do it. And you've already shown up by reading this book.

APPENDIX

USEFUL TIPS AND INFORMATION

STAYING SAFE DURING PROTESTS

Most movements advocate peaceful protesting, which is an activity protected by the Human Rights Act. But these situations are often dynamic and fast-changing, so you need to keep your wits about you.

Before you arrive at the protest, make a plan with your companions. Where will you meet if you get separated? What time? Who should they call if there's an emergency? Make sure everyone in your group is clear about what to do if things don't go as anticipated.

What to bring

First of all, make sure you come well prepared. A rucksack or cross-body bag will allow you to move freely and should include:

- Water, ideally in a bottle with a squirty top so you can wash your skin or eyes if necessary.
- Energy snacks – think protein bars and granola rather than sugary stuff that will make you feel lethargic.
- Enough cash for a pay phone or public transport home.
- A basic first-aid kit.
- A phone-charging bank, so you don't run out of juice.
- Medicines such as inhalers, EpiPens or insulin.
- A hat, bandana or sunglasses. These will shield you from the elements as well as obscure your face from surveillance and protect your privacy.
- ID, or if you're not comfortable taking identification, details of an emergency contact.

When you're there

Stay alert and engaged with your surroundings.

- Look out for things that don't seem right, and document them if you feel safe to do so.
- Watch for signs of panic or excessive aggression in others.
- Help those around you – offer water if you have extra, or hold their things while they tie their shoes.
- If violence breaks out, move quickly and calmly to the edge of the crowd, but don't run. Running draws attention to yourself and could incite a panic.

Know your rights

Get clued-up on your rights before you go, so you have the law on your side if something goes wrong. Don't resist arrest even if what's happening is unfair – instead, make a note of the arresting officer. If you witness someone else being arrested, you have a right to film it.

- You don't have to answer police questions. It's often safer to respond with 'no comment' to their queries until you have legal assistance.
- You don't have to give police your personal details.
- Ask 'Under what power?' to challenge police to act lawfully – some officers will rely on you not knowing the law. Ask them what law they are using and why, and make a note of what was said and by whom as soon as possible.
- Do not feel pressured into accepting a caution. Offering you a caution is a way of getting you to admit guilt without having to charge you, which means they don't have to provide any evidence of wrongdoing. At the very least, don't accept a caution without taking advice from a solicitor familiar with protest matters.

STOP AND SEARCH

The police power of 'stop and search' was first introduced to the UK in 1984, and has proved to be a controversial issue ever since. According to data from the Home Office, a black person is nine times more likely to be stopped and searched than a white person.[135] If you're stopped and searched, whether at a protest or anywhere else, it's important you know your rights.

Police are only able to search you if they have 'reasonable grounds' to believe you're carrying:

- Illegal drugs
- A weapon
- Stolen property
- Something which could be used to commit a crime

If stopped by police, you must comply – however, they must legally:

- Tell you who they are and give you their badge number
- Say why they are stopping you and under what law
- Tell you what they expect to find on you
- Give you a receipt of the search or tell you how to get one

An officer can ask you to remove gloves, a jacket or coat. Anything else – including religious clothing – must be done out of public view, and the search conducted by someone of the same sex as you.

You are allowed to film the stop and search, as long as you don't obstruct it. If you want to make a complaint about the search, the police officer must give you details on how to do so.

The laws in England and Wales are slightly different to those in Scotland; https://www.gov.uk/police-powers-to-stop-and-search-your-rights tells you how stop and search operates in your area.

The US, meanwhile, operates a policy called 'stop and frisk', which is largely similar to the UK's initiative. Learn about your rights in the States here: https://www.acludc.org/en/know-your-rights/know-your-rights-stop-and-frisk.

AVOIDING FAKE NEWS

Fake news is a major problem. Tech giants such as Facebook, Twitter and Google are all taking steps to control the issue, but because we're at such a polarising point in history – and because social media makes it so easy to share – it's probably going to get worse before it gets better.

There are two kinds of fake news:

1. False stories deliberately published or shared to make people believe something that's untrue.
2. Stories that *may* have some truth to them but are not completely accurate.

Both types of story have the power to cause harm by galvanising echo chambers, causing mass panic, propagating dangerous information, deepening political and social divides, and weakening trust in reputable media sources.

And fake news isn't always easy to spot – if something looks credible, or at the very least aligns with beliefs that someone holds dear to them, it only takes a few clicks to push that disinformation out further into the world.

Check the following before hitting the share button:

- Think critically. Fake news is often written in such a way that it's believable, or conversely, for shock value that elicits a strong instinctive reaction, such as fear or anger. Ask yourself, 'Why has this story been written? Is it trying to persuade me of a certain viewpoint?'
- Check the source. Is the story from a reputable site? If it's hosted on a site you've never heard of before, or which has an unusual web extension, such as, 'infonet' or '.newsnow' instead of '.com' or '.co.uk', then it might be suspect.

- Google the story. This takes about five seconds and will tell you if any other sites are reporting the news. Professional global news agencies such as Reuters, CNN and the BBC have rigorous editorial guidelines in place, so if they're reporting the story, it's probably legit.
- Look at the evidence. A credible news story will contain facts, data and quotes from named experts. Stories that rely on anecdotes or vague 'sources' should be questioned.
- Don't take images at face value. Anyone who owns a smartphone is capable of basic picture editing, and it's not difficult to put random text over an image pulled off the internet. Be critical of politically tinged memes that get sent around Facebook and WhatsApp – the pictures they use might be completely accurate but used in entirely the wrong context. Google Reverse Image Search is your friend!
- Remember that spoof sites such as *The Onion* and *The Daily Mash* exist, which can confuse things if satire isn't your strong suit.

STAYING SAFE ONLINE

Many of us grew up with the advent of the internet or were born into an already digital world, so it's easy to just assume we're clued-up when it comes to online safety. We know not to click big flashing links promising immediate weight loss, and that the Nigerian prince offering us millions of dollars in exchange for a small 'equity release payment' probably isn't real.

But as hackers and hacking tech is becoming more sophisticated, the measures we've taken for granted in the past just don't cut it any more. For example, back in 2000, the password 'security1' would have taken three years and ten months to crack. By 2016, it was just three months. Today, it's milliseconds.[136]

Of course, passwords exist to protect sensitive information that we don't want to share with others, but the stuff we *do* share comes with its own problems. We live such a huge part of our lives online now, sharing details like birthdays and addresses, and unknowingly announcing sensitive information that can be used against us. Take those memes that say things like 'Your first pet's name and your mother's maiden name equals your stripper name! Lol!' As soon as you respond with 'Binky Laithwaite' or whatever amusingly apt answer you arrive at, you've basically given any bad actors that might be lurking about a skeleton key to your personal stuff, since so many platforms rely on you telling them this info to prove your identity or reset passwords and so on.

So as tech-savvy as you might be, it's always worth setting aside some time now and then to make sure you're running a tight ship.

- Everyone knows that passwords need to be complex and unique to every site or platform you use, but who has the time – or the brain capacity – for that? A password manager will look after that for you, suggesting strong passwords and auto-filling them where necessary – and you can sync it between your phone and other devices, such as a laptop or PC, so the process is pretty seamless.
- Change your passwords regularly. Just because you've got a super-complex password doesn't mean it's impossible to crack, and determined hackers will have their tech grinding away in the background for as long as it takes to figure it out. Update them every three months or so.
- If a platform or website encourages you to use two-factor authentication (2FA) – which offers an additional layer of protection by requiring a fingerprint unlock or code input – then use it.

- Use reputable antivirus security software that includes a firewall – this is an electronic 'barrier' that blocks unauthorised access to your devices.
- Be smart about what you share online and how you share it. Be mindful of privacy settings, geotagging, social media check-ins and so on, as well as the content itself. If you can think of a way that what you're about to share could be used nefariously, you're better off just giving it a swerve.

DOXING

The term 'doxing' (or 'doxxing') comes from the expression 'dropping dox', a revenge tactic used by hackers when they would reveal malicious information about a rival. Today, though, anyone can be a victim, with nasty types – usually trolls that don't like what someone has to say – uncovering sensitive personal information and publishing it online. This includes things like addresses, bank details, places of work, details about family members, nudes and so on.

This is harder to do if you're strict about your online security, of course, and the chances of it happening to you are pretty slim. But some of these miserable creatures are very highly skilled and bafflingly determined, and clearly don't have a whole lot else going on in their sad lives.

Being doxed is stressful, upsetting and can leave you feeling overwhelmed and helpless. But don't panic, take a deep breath and then take action.

- If you feel like you're in immediate danger, call your local emergency number and explain the situation. If you feel unsafe where you are, move somewhere else.
- Tell someone you trust, so you're not dealing with it alone.
- Document the evidence – take screenshots of everything, ideally including the time or date, as well as the website URL.
- Report the harassment to whatever platform your information appears on. Sites like Facebook, Reddit and Twitter have terms-of-service agreements to prevent this kind of misuse.
- Lockdown your accounts – change your passwords and consider making your profiles private for the time being. In the longer term, you might want to think about changing your phone number, usernames or any other identifying information.
- Information spreads quickly online, so even if the sensitive information is taken down from its original location, it may still be available elsewhere. Set a Google alert for your name and any related

keywords, and consider enlisting the help of a monitoring service. Many security software companies offer services that will scan the dark web and alert you if any of your personal information has been exposed there.

USEFUL WEBSITES

BAME

Diversity UK: diversityuk.org
NAACP: naacp.org (US)
Runnymede: runnymedetrust.org

DISABILITIES

Dreamscape: dreamscapefoundation.org (US)
Mencap: mencap.org.uk
Sense: sense.org.uk
Scope: scope.org.uk

DRUGS AND ALCOHOL MISUSE

Addiction Center: addictioncenter.com (US)
FRANK: talktofrank.com
We Are With You: wearewithyou.org.uk

FOOD POVERTY

Feeding America: feedingamerica.org (US)
The Trussell Trust: trusselltrust.org

HOUSING

National Housing Law Project: nhlp.org (US)
Shelter: shelter.org.uk

IMMIGRATION AND ASYLUM

American Immigration Council:
americanimmigrationcouncil.org (US)
Migrant Help UK: migranthelpuk.org

LEGAL ADVICE

Citizens Advice: citizensadvice.org.uk
Legal aid: usa.gov/legal-aid (US)

LGBTQ+

LGBT Foundation: lgbt.foundation
Stonewall: stonewall.org.uk
The Center: gaycenter.org (US)

LOCAL POLITICS

Common Cause: commoncause.org (US)
They Work For You: theyworkforyou.com

MENTAL HEALTH

Crisis Text Line: crisistextline.org (US)
Mind: mind.org.uk
Rethink: rethink.org

SEXUAL HEALTH/REPRODUCTION

Brook: brook.org.uk
Marie Stopes UK: mariestopes.org.uk
Planned Parenthood: plannedparenthood.org (US)

WOMEN

Fawcett Society: fawcettsociety.org.uk
National Organization for Women: now.org (US)
Women's Aid: womensaid.org.uk

GLOSSARY

HELPFUL EXPLAINERS

ALGORITHM

A set of instructions designed to perform a specific task. In computing – or more specifically, social media – an algorithm is designed to carry out a function, such as showing you people you may know or content that you might be interested in based on your previous online activity.

ALLY

A person who is united with a wider cause even if they themselves may not be directly affected by it. For example, being a queer or feminist ally means you support the endeavours and experiences of LGBTQ+ individuals or women without being queer or a woman yourself.

BIAS

An inclination or prejudice towards a person or group of people. A bias can be favourable or unfavourable, but typically has negative connotations when used to refer to marginalised groups, such as 'racial bias' or 'gender bias'.

BOOMERS

The name given to the generation of people born between 1946 and 1964, during the post-Second-World-War baby boom.

CARBON DIOXIDE/CO_2

A heat-trapping (greenhouse) gas, which is released through human activities as well as natural processes such as respiration and volcanic eruptions. Human activity has been responsible for a massive increase in CO_2 production, which is driving climate change.

CARBON FOOTPRINT

The measure of the impact your activities have on the amount of carbon produced through burning fossil fuels. It's expressed as a weight of CO_2 emissions in tonnes.

CLEAN ENERGY

Energy that's derived from alternative sources to fossil fuels – typically green, zero-emissions sources, such as the wind or sun. The term is often used interchangeably with 'renewable energy' or 'green energy'.

CLIMATE CHANGE/CRISIS

At its basic level, the term 'climate change' is used to describe a change in average climatic conditions – such as temperature and rainfall – over a long period of time. Over the last several decades, however, changes have been taking place rapidly, which scientists attribute to increased carbon dioxide emissions from humanity's activities. This has resulted in higher temperatures, more extreme weather and melting polar ice, which – if left unchecked – will have a devastating impact on the planet, hence the increasing use of the term 'climate crisis'. Climate scientists agree that we must limit temperature rises to 1.5°C to avoid the worst consequences of climate change.

CSR

Corporate social responsibility: a management concept where companies integrate social and environmental concerns into their business operations.

DEFORESTATION

A term used to describe the rapid decrease in forest and woodland areas around the world because of human activities such as agriculture, manufacturing, urbanisation and mining.

ECHO CHAMBER

An environment – usually online – where a person will only encounter opinions and beliefs that coincide with their own. This means that existing views are generally reinforced, and alternative ideas and ways of thinking are ignored or criticised.

ECOSYSTEM

A community of living creatures – plants and animals (and humans, too) – that exist in a particular region. Each 'member' of the ecosystem interacts with one another and non-living parts of the environment in ways that result in important functions, such as helping to purify the air or pollinate crops. Coral reefs, deserts and rainforests are examples of ecosystems. Disrupting their delicate balance can have serious repercussions for the wider environment.

EMISSIONS

The catch-all term used to describe the gases and particles released into the atmosphere that can have an impact on the health of the planet. 'Carbon emissions' is probably the most common use of the term.

ENERGY EFFICIENCY

Using less energy to perform the same task. Say you've got two largely identical fridge freezers. They're both doing the same job, but if one is using less energy than the other, then it is more energy efficient. In a nutshell, energy efficiency is about doing the same or more with less.

FOSSIL FUELS

Fossil fuels are naturally occurring resources such as coal, crude oil and natural gas, so-named because they come from the fossilised, buried remains of plants and animals that lived millions of years ago. People have traditionally relied on burning these fuels to generate energy for everything from cars to heating. But because of their origins, they have a high carbon content, so they are a major contributor to climate change. They are also finite – once we've used up all the world's oil and coal, it will be gone forever.

GEN Z

Generation Z: the generation of people born between 1996 and 2015.

GLOBAL WARMING

The gradual increase in the overall temperature of the earth's atmosphere, resulting in an enhanced green-house effect, which is generally attributed to increasing greenhouse gas emissions, such as carbon dioxide. An increasingly warm planet is what is driving the climate crisis.

GREEN ENERGY

Energy that's derived from alternative sources to fossil fuels – typically clean, zero-emissions sources, such as the wind or sun. The term is often used interchangeably with 'renewable energy' or 'clean energy'.

GREENHOUSE EFFECT/GASES

The greenhouse effect is a natural process that keeps the earth's surface warm. When energy from the sun reaches the earth's atmosphere, some of it is reflected back into space and some of it is absorbed by the land and oceans. This heat then radiates towards space, and some of it is trapped by greenhouse gases in the atmosphere, keeping the planet warm enough to sustain life. So it's kind of important! These greenhouse gases include water vapour, carbon dioxide, methane and nitrous oxide, which are both naturally occurring and produced by humans. The problem is, an increasing volume of human-produced greenhouse gases means that the heat that would otherwise radiate back into space is becoming trapped in our atmosphere, causing the earth's temperature to rise (global warming), and subsequently driving climate change.

LANDFILL

Also known as a 'dump', landfill is where waste and disposable materials are stored. Landfill sites are usually massive holes or excavated pits in the ground, which are covered over when full. They produce a lot of methane – a dangerous greenhouse gas that contributes to climate change – and can cause damage to nearby land and waterways as toxic material often leaches out of these sites. Anything that can't be reused or recycled (or recyclable materials that have been contaminated) will end up in landfill.

LOBBYING

An attempt by individuals or groups to influence the decisions of government and other policymakers. The term's origins come from historical efforts to sway the votes of officials in the lobby area outside legislative chambers.

MARGINALISED

A person or group of people that is often treated as unimportant, insignificant or of a lower status, and that are denied full access to mainstream social, political and economic activities.

MICROPLASTICS

Very small pieces of plastic, less than 5mm long, that end up in the environment (usually in waterways) as a result of the disposal and breakdown of consumer products and litter.

MILLENNIAL

Millennials: the generation of people born between 1981 and 1996.

NATURAL RESOURCES

Things that exist on the planet independently of human interference, such as sunlight, water, plants, trees, animals and fossil fuels.

ORGANIC

There's no universally agreed definition for the term 'organic', since different countries and organisations have their own governance on the label. Generally speaking, however, it refers to food (and other items such as cotton or skincare products) grown and produced without artificial fertilisers and using fewer pesticides than typical methods.

High animal welfare standards are also an important part of the organics ethos.

PLANT-BASED

Plant-based food is food that comes directly from the earth, such as fruit and veg, nuts, seeds, oils, whole grains and beans.

POLLUTION

Anything that's introduced to the environment that is dirty, unclean or has a harmful effect.

RECYCLING

The process of turning used or waste materials into new materials that can be reused. Aluminium cans and tins can be recycled into new cans and tins, which means new aluminium doesn't have to be mined to create another product. Paper, meanwhile, can be recycled to save trees being cut down for 'brand new' or 'virgin' paper.

RENEWABLE ENERGY

Energy that's derived from alternative sources to fossil fuels – typically clean and abundant sources, such as the wind or sun. The term is often used interchangeably with 'green energy' or 'clean energy'.

SHARING ECONOMY

A system – sometimes officially managed but often casual and ungoverned – where individuals share goods and services, therefore mitigating the need to use up existing resources to produce further goods and services. Borrowing a neighbour's drill or ridesharing with a friend are examples of sharing economy practices.

SLACKTIVISM

Sometimes called 'armchair activism', the term is used to describe the action of supporting a political or social cause while exerting very little effort – by signing an online petition or sharing a relevant news article on social media, for example. It's often used in a derogatory manner, but slacktivism has its place in the wider activism jigsaw! (See also pages 9–11).

SOCIAL CAPITAL

The social and cultural cohesiveness of a society, derived through trust and shared identity and values. The higher a community's social capital, the better they are able to work together to achieve a common purpose or goal.

SUSTAINABILITY

The process and action through which humankind uses natural resources and treats the planet so that the quality of life for future generations doesn't decrease.

WASTE

Typically used to describe materials bound for landfill, but waste is a verb, too. To waste something is to consume it recklessly, without thought and consideration, or without an adequate 'pay-off'.

NOTES

INTRODUCTION

1. Chenoweth, Erica, 'The Success of Nonviolent Civil Resistance', ICNC, *Tedx*, 2013
2. 'How to Get the Most Out Of Your Kitchen Appliances', *Energy Saving Trust*, 2017
3. 'Greenhouse Gas Equivalencies Calculator', *US EPA*, 2020

IF YOU HAVE FIVE MINUTES …

4. 'Search Engine Market Share', *Netmarketshare.Com*, 2020
5. 'Google Search Statistics', *Internet Live Stats*, 2020
6. 'Google: Ad Revenue 2001–2018', *Statista*, 2020
7. 'Raise Money For Charity When You Search The Web', *Everyclick.Com*, 2020
8. 'Micro-Donations Matter', *Pennies*, 2020
9. Mohsin, Maryam, '10 Online Shopping Statistics You Need to Know In 2021', *Oberlo*, 2020
10. 'You Shop. Your Cause Gets Money. For Free', *Easyfundraising*, 2020

11. 'UK Small Business Statistics', *Fsb.org.uk*, 2020
12. Morse, Amyas, 'Government's Spending With Small and Medium-sized Enterprises', National Audit Office, 2016
13. Shahmohammadi, Sadegh *et al.*, 'Comparative Greenhouse Gas Footprinting of Online versus Traditional Shopping for Fast-Moving Consumer Goods: A Stochastic Approach', *Environmental Science & Technology*, 2020
14. Bushwick, Sophie, 'Delivery from Local Store Is Greenest Shopping Method – Most of the Time', *Scientific American*, 2020
15. Smith, Alison *et al.*, 'The Validity of Food Miles as an Indicator of Sustainable Development', DEFRA, 2005
16. Pretty, J. *et al.*, 'Farm Costs and Food Miles: An Assessment of the Full Cost of the UK Weekly Food Basket', *Food Policy*, 2005
17. 'Our Aim Is to End Hunger and Poverty In the UK', *The Trussell Trust*, 2020
18. Armstrong, Martin, 'The US Leads the World in Toilet Paper Consumption', *Statistica*, 2018
19. 'Why Toilet Paper is Bad for the Environment', *Brondell*, 2018
20. 'Greenhouse Gas Equivalencies Calculator', *US EPA*, 2020
21. 'Toilet Paper', *Ethical Consumer*, 2020
22. 'Batteries', *Recycle More*, 2020

23. 'Batteries Recycling', *First Mile*, 2020
24. 'Duracell Rechargeable AAA 750mAh Batteries', *Duracell*, 2020
25. Niinimäki, Kirsi *et al.*, 'The Environmental Price of Fast Fashion', *Nature Reviews Earth & Environment*, 2020
26. McFall-Johnsen, Morgan, 'These Facts Show How Unsustainable the Fashion Industry Is', World Economic Forum, 2020
27. Drew, Deborah, 'The Apparel Industry's Environmental Impact in 6 Graphics', *World Resources Institute*, 2017
28. 'Facts and Figures about Materials, Waste and Recycling', *EPA*, 2020
29. 'One Garbage Truck of Textiles Wasted Every Second: Report Creates Vision for Change', *Ellen MacArthur Foundation*, 2017
30. Remy, Nathalie, 'Style That's Sustainable: A New Fast-fashion Formula', *McKinsey & Company*, 2016
31. 'A New Textiles Economy: Redesigning Fashion's Future', *Ellen MacArthur Foundation*, 2017
32. 'A New Textiles Economy: Redesigning Fashion's Future', *Ellen MacArthur Foundation*, 2017
33. 'Tips to Reduce Junk Mail', *Veolia*, 2020
34. 'The Fifth Carbon Budget. How Every Household Can Help Reduce the UK's Carbon Footprint', Committee on Climate Change, 2016

35. Lerman, Susannah, 'Lazy Lawn Mowers Can Help Support Suburban Bee Populations and Diversity', *University of Massachusetts Amherst*, 2018
36. 'CO2 Emissions From Cars: Facts and Figures', *European Parliament*, 2019
37. Johnson, David, 'Michelin Warns Fleets on Cost of Driving on Under-inflated Tyres', *Michelin*, 2017
38. 'Green Driving Tips', *The Ethical Choice*, 2020
39. 'Save Fuel and Money with Eco-driving', *The AA*, 2017
40. 'Engine Idling – Why It's So Harmful and What's Being Done', *RAC*, 2020
41. 'How Clean Is England? The Local Environmental Quality Survey of England 2014/15', Keep Britain Tidy, 2015
42. 'The Wider Cost of Litter: A Summary Paper', Keep Britain Tidy, 2014
43. 'Contamination of Recycling by Food or General Waste', *Gov.uk*, 2019
44. McMunn, Anne *et al.*, 'Gender Divisions of Paid and Unpaid Work In Contemporary UK Couples', *Work, Employment and Society*, 2019
45. Hess, Cynthia *et al.*, 'Providing Unpaid Household and Care Work In the United States: Uncovering Inequality', *Institute for Women's Policy Research*, 2020
46. 'Women Shoulder the Responsibility of Unpaid Work', *Office for National Statistics*, 2016

47. Lin, Ying, '10 Twitter Statistics Every Marketer Should Know In 2021', *Oberlo*, 2020

IF YOU HAVE AN HOUR ...

48. 'Average Brit Will Emit More By 12 January Than Residents of Seven African Countries do In a Year', *Oxfam*, 2020
49. 'Carbon Monoxide Poisoning Sends 4,000 People to A&E Each Year', *Gov.uk*, 2011
50. 'How Much Money Can a New Boiler Really Save Me?', *Hometree*, 2020
51. 'Draught-proofing', *Energy Saving Trust*, 2020
52. Paraskevakos, T., 'Patent Sensor Monitoring Device'. US3842208A, United States Patent and Trademark Office, 15 October 1974
53. 'Smart Meters and Energy Usage: A Survey of Energy Behaviour Among Those Who Have Had a Smart Meter, and Those Who Have Yet to Get One', *Smart Energy GB*, 2019
54. 'Smart Meter Statistics in Great Britain: Quarterly Report to End March 2020', *Department for Business, Energy and Industrial Strategy*, 2020
55. 'Greenhouse Gas Equivalencies Calculator', *US EPA*, 2020
56. 'Lighting', *Energy Saving Trust*, 2020
57. 'CFLs vs. LEDs: The Better Bulbs', *Green America*, 2020

58. 'Why We Should All be Saving Water', *Energy Saving Trust*, 2020
59. 'Save Water With Hippo', *Hippo the Water Saver*, 2013
60. 'What's In Your Burger? More Than You Think', *UN Environment Programme*, 2018
61. Poore, J., 'Reducing Food's Environmental Impacts Through Producers and Consumers', *Science*, 2018
62. 'EU Climate Diet: 71 Per Cent Less Meat by 2030', *Greenpeace*, 2020
63. 'The Benefits of Meatless Monday', *Monday Campaigns*, 2020
64. Meyer, Nanna, 'Sustainability Integration Into Nutrition for Exercise and Sport', *Nutrients*, 2017
65. 'Global Food Losses and Food Waste', *Food and Agriculture Organization of the United Nations*, 2011
66. 'Food Losses and Waste in the Context of Sustainable Food Systems', *HLPE*, 2014
67. Song, Xiao-Peng *et al.*, 'Global Land Change From 1982 to 2016', *Nature*, 2018
68. 'Why Plant Trees?', *Woodland Trust*, 2020
69. 'Why Should the UK Double Tree Cover?', *Friends of the Earth*, 2020
70. 'Hectares of Forests Cut Down or Burned', *The World Counts*, 2020
71. Allain, Rhett, 'If Each of Us Planted a Tree, Would It Slow Global Warming?' *Wired*, 2019

72. 'Big Garden Birdwatch results', *RSPB*, 2020
73. 'What We Do', *British Red Cross*, 2020
74. 'No One Should Have No One', *Age UK*, 2017
75. 'Shocking Extent of Loneliness Faced by Young Mothers Revealed', *Co-operative*, 2018
76. 'Loneliness', *Sense*, 2020
77. 'Loneliness Increases Risk of Premature Death', *NHS*, 2015
78. 'History and Background Information', *Freecycle*, 2020
79. 'Freegle Stats', *Freegle*, 2020
80. 'Charity Shops FAQs', *Charity Retail Association*, 2020
81. 'Five Good Reasons to Support Your Local Charity Shops', *Wandsworth Oasis*, 2020
82. 'Charity Shop Volunteering', *Charity Retail Association*, 2020
83. Cipriani, Val, '30 per cent of People Think Charity Shops Are More Important to Society After Crisis', *Civil Society News*, 2020
84. 'Written Evidence We Received During the Investigation Into Single-use Plastics: Unflushables', London Assembly, 2018
85. 'How Much Plastic is in Period Pads?', *Natracare*, 2020
86. 'Why Switch?', *Bloom and Nora*, 2020
87. 'HSBC to Help Combat Climate Change With a $100 Billion Boost for Sustainable Financing', *HSBC*, 2017
88. 'Dig Deeper: Fossil Bank Financing By Client', *Rainforest Action Network*, 2020

89. 'Banking on Climate Change: Fossil Fuel Finance Report 2019', *Rainforest Alliance Network*, 2019
90. 'Banking on Climate Change: Fossil Fuel Finance Report 2020', *Rainforest Alliance Network*, 2020
91. Grattan, Ed, 'Socially Responsible Investing Market on Cusp of Momentus Growth (173 Per Cent)', *Triodus*, 2018
92. 'New Survey Reveals 75 Per Cent of Millennials Expect Employers to Take a Stand on Social Issues', *Glassdoor*, 2017
93. McQueen, Nina, 'Workplace Culture Trends: The Key to Hiring (and Keeping) Top Talent in 2018', *LinkedIn*, 2018
94. 'Employee Activism in the Age of Purpose: Employees (Up)rising', *Weber Shandwick*, 2019
95. 'The New World of Work: Report Warns of an Inprecedented Rise in Workplace Activism', *Herbert Smith Freehills*, 2019
96. Boccalandro, Bea, 'Increasing Employee Engagement Through Corporate Volunteering', *Voluntare*, 2018
97. Rochlin, Steve *et al.*, 'Defining the Competitive and Financial Advantages of Corporate Responsibility and Sustainability', *IO Sustainability and the Lewis Institute for Social Innovation at Babson College*, 2015
98. Lee, S. J. and Reeves, T. C., 'Edgar Dale: A Significant Contributor to the Field of Educational Technology', *Educational Technology*, 2007

99. 'Recycling Bill Success: How We Got the UK Recycling', *Friends of the Earth*, 2016
100. 'Why Should I Vote in the General Election?', *Voting Counts*, 2019
101. 'EU Referendum Results', *BBC*, 2016

IF YOU HAVE A DAY ...

102. Greep, Monica, 'No Cash in the Attic! Homeowners Have an Average of £2,600 in Unwanted Items Stored Away, eBay Reveals', *Daily Mail*, 2020
103. Ivanova, Diana *et al.*, 'Environmental Impact Assessment of Household Consumption', *Journal of Industrial Ecology*, 2015
104. 'Roof and Loft Insulation', *Energy Saving Trust*, 2020
105. 'Greenhouse Gas Equivalencies Calculator', *US EPA*, 2020
106. 'Greenhouse Gas Equivalencies Calculator', *US EPA*, 2020
107. 'Garden Trends Report 2018', *Wyevale Garden Centres*, 2018
108. 'How Can Your Garden Reduce Your Stress Levels?', *The American Institute of Stress*, 2019
109. 'Garden Trends Report 2018', *Wyevale Garden Centres*, 2018
110. 'What is the Economic Contribution of the Voluntary Sector?', *NCVO*, 2018

111. '70 Years of Life Saving Blood Donations', *NHS Blood and Transplant*, 2016
112. 'Why Give Blood', *NHS Blood and Transplant*, 2020
113. Hurd, Noelle and Zimmerman, Marc, 'Role Models', *Encyclopedia of Adolescence*, 2011
114. 'Company Facts', *Ancestry*, 2020
115. 'Are Prehospital Deaths From Trauma and Accidental Injury Preventable? A Summary Report', *British Red Cross*, 2016
116. Park, C. *et al.*, 'The Impact of Sustained Engagement on Cognitive Function in Older Adults: The Synapse Project', *Psychol Sci*, 2014
117. 'The Costs and Benefits of UK World Heritage Site Status', *Department for Culture, Media and Sport*, 2007
118. O'Connor, Anahad, 'The Claim: Exposure to Plants and Parks Can Boost Immunity', *New York Times*, 2010
119. Steakley, Lia, 'Having Trouble Sleeping? Research Suggests Spending More Time Outdoors', *Stanford Medicine*, 2015
120. Wang, Shirley, 'Coffee Break? Walk in the Park? Why Unwinding is Hard', *The Wall Street Journal*, 2011
121. Wu, Pei-Chang *et al.*, 'Outdoor Activity During Class Recess Reduces Myopia Onset and Progression in School Children', *Ophthalmology*, 2013
122. Richardson, Miles *et al.*, '30 Days Wild: Development and Evaluation of a Large-Scale Nature Engagement Campaign to Improve Well-Being', *PLoS ONE*, 2016

123. Genevive, R. Meredith *et al.*, 'Minimum Time Dose in Nature to Positively Impact the Mental Health of College-Aged Students, and How to Measure It: A Scoping Review', *Frontiers in Psychology*, 2020
124. Suttie, Jill, 'How Nature Can Make You Kinder, Happier and More Creative', *Greater Good Magazine*, 2016
125. '10 Shocking Facts About Plastic', *National Geographic*, 2020
126. '10 Shocking Facts About Plastic', *National Geographic*, 2020
127. 'Plastic Pollution – Facts and Figures', *Surfers Against Sewage*, 2020
128. Parker, Laura, 'Beach Clean-up Study Shows Global Scope of Plastic Pollution', *National Geographic*, 2018
129. Bennett, T. L., *et al.*, 'The Effectiveness of Neighbourhood Watch', *Security Journal*, 2009
130. 'Research and Reports', *Groundwork*, 2020
131. 'Local Community', *Action for Happiness*, 2020
132. Horowitz, Juliana and Livingston, Gretchen, 'How Americans View the Black Lives Matter Movement', *Pew Research Center*, 2016
133. Parker, Kim *et al.*, 'Amid Protests, Majorities Across Racial and Ethnic Groups Express Support for the Black Lives Matter Movement', *Pew Research Center*, 2020

134. McCormick, Tyler H. *et al.*, 'How Many People Do You Know?: Efficiently Estimating Personal Network Size', *Journal of the American Statistical Association*, 2010

APPENDIX

135. 'What is Stop and Search and What Are My Rights?', *BBC*

136. 'Estimating Password Cracking Times', *Better Buys*, 2015